FOUNTAIN SHELTON MAY

A History of a Civil War Soldier

Flora McCarty

Fountain Shelton May
A History of a Civil War Soldier
By Flora McCarty

Copyright © 2011

Copyright © 2017 - Revised Edition

All Rights Reserved. No part of this book may be reproduced or transmitted in any form or by any means, electronic or mechanical, including photocopying, faxing, recording, emailing, posting on social media or by any information storage and retrieval system, or used for any other purpose without written permission from the author.

Published by Blue Spruce Publishing Company
2175 Golf Isle Drive, Suite 1024
Melbourne, FL 32935
877-346-2667
info@BlueSprucePublishing.com

Cover Photo: Original photo owned by the author that was passed down through the generations. Please refer to the Illustration References for information on photos used in this book.

ISBN: 978-1-943581-06-1

Table of Contents

Introduction	iv
About the Author	vi
Early Life	1
Military	5
Prisoner of War	15
The Noble Twenty-Third	25
Military Records	29
Widow's Pension	31
War Monument, Milan, Missouri	39
Soldiers from Sullivan County, Missouri	41
Men held at Camp Oglethorpe	49
POWs at Battle of Shiloh	51
Shiloh National Military Park	59
Chain of Command	61
Ulysses S. Grant	67
Family of Fountain Shelton May	71
Parents and Siblings of Fountain Shelton May	79
Ancestors of Fountain Shelton May	87
Lineage Chart	88
Y-DNA Report	89
Pedigree Chart	90
Adam May	91
Johann Bott	94
Revolutionary War Patriot Lawrence Raynes	95
Bibliography	105
Illustration References	106

INTRODUCTION

I've known of the existence of Fountain Shelton May for several years but never given him much study. As his great-great-granddaughter, I first learned of him as I looked at the old photos in my mother's trunk of pictures. There I found the old daguerreotype that had Fountain May looking out at me. I learned that he had been prisoner and died in a prison camp. Beyond that, I'd never taken time to investigate, for whatever reason, mostly lack of time, but also because the details never seemed important.

I held the pension application of Virginia May in my hands at the Washington, D.C., National Archives several years ago. It was an amazing experience. To my delight, I was handed the original paperwork – some on Big Chief paper – that Virginia had filled out so many years ago. The thought of her touching those same papers was humbling. But I was not looking, at that time, for information about Fountain. Mainly I was interested, then, in finding out more about his family. So even then, I neglected Fountain May.

A few years ago, however, my cousins and I visited Sullivan County, Missouri where Fountain and his family lived. There, on the lawn of the courthouse, and much to our delight, was a war memorial upon which Fountain's name was inscribed. We did our planned research and then visited the gravesite of his wife, Virginia. Nearby was the grave of Thomas J. Dunlap, son of James T. Dunlap, who had enrolled Fountain May as a soldier in 1861. Suddenly, I was hooked. I had to find out more about Fountain Shelton May. After all, he was my grandmother's grandfather. He seemed a little more real to me now.

Beyond the photograph, few family records existed. So here, in this writing, I have relied on other accounts of what happened and tried to find places and times where Fountain would have been.

Details of Fountain's early life are still sketchy. We know the name of his parents, Jacob and Elizabeth May, and the names of his brothers and sisters. We also know where the May family is from, and that he had at least two Revolutionary War Patriots in his family (Christian May and Lawrence Raynes). But there is little information about his daily life in Virginia beyond dates and locations.

The account of Fountain's prison experience is taken largely from F. F. Kiner's One Year's Soldiering, written soon after his release in 1863. Although Chaplain Kiner was part of an Iowa unit, he was captured at Shiloh alongside those of the 23rd Missouri Infantry, and was taken to the same prison where Fountain May was held. His experiences were undoubtedly almost identical to Fountain's. How fortunate we are that Chaplain Kiner was able to record his experience so vividly.

My purpose for this writing is to help other people see Fountain Shelton May as a real person and to honor his remarkable service to our country. What a terrible price he paid to preserve the union of these United States of America!

May you enjoy this detailed account of Fountain Shelton May, and know my enjoyment of sharing it with you.

Flora McCarty
Author and Great-Great-Granddaughter of Fountain Shelton May
Aurora, Colorado 2011

ABOUT THE AUTHOR

Flora McCarty is the Great-Great-Granddaughter of Fountain Shelton May. She has been researching family history for 35 years. She is a member of the Daughters of American Revolution (DAR) since 2011, and has written books on her ancestors in both the American Revolution and the Civil War. A graduate of State University of New York (Albany), Flora makes her home in Colorado.

EARLY LIFE

Rockingham County, Virginia was created in 1778 from part of Augusta County. Fountain's grandparents, Adam and Elizabeth May, of German heritage[1], came to Rockingham County about 1791 from Pennsylvania. Rockingham County is in the heart of the beautiful Shenandoah Valley where the Shenandoah National Park is now located. The early Native Americans who lived in this region called it Shenandoah, which means "daughter of the stars." There are many spectacular limestone caverns in the area and rock formations which resemble chimneys, towering 120 feet above the ground floor. The Shenandoah River runs the through this picturesque area. Fountain's father, Jacob May, was a miller. He probably operated his mill along this river to provide flour for the local citizenry.

Generally speaking Rockingham and Augusta Counties were predominately populated with the Scots-Irish and Germans. About 57 percent of the population of Rockingham County was German. The Scots-Irish seem to have settled more in Augusta County and southward, and the Germans from Rockingham County north. Many of the settlers came down from Pennsylvania through the Great Valley, a 200 mile long valley nestled between the Blue Ridge and the Allegheny mountains. The road through the valley was open to wagon traffic by 1765 and Fountain's grandfather, Adam May, followed the road to Rockingham County sometime before 1791.

An example of a Grist Mill

Fountain's family lived in Rockingham County at the same time as Abraham Lincoln's early family. Lincoln's great-grandfather, John Lincoln, died in Rockingham County in 1788. His

---

[1] Per DNA testing (see ancestry)

uncle, Jacob Lincoln, built a house in Rockingham County in 1800 and lived there for many years with his family.[2]

Fountain Shelton May was born Nov 16, 1825 in Rockingham County and grew up in this beautiful area. He had eleven siblings, 6 brothers and 5 sisters; he was the second child and the second son. He never learned to read or write.[3] It is possible that he had to work in the mill, helping his father to support the family, instead of going to school. There were schools in Rockingham County during that time, so it's not known why he didn't attend.

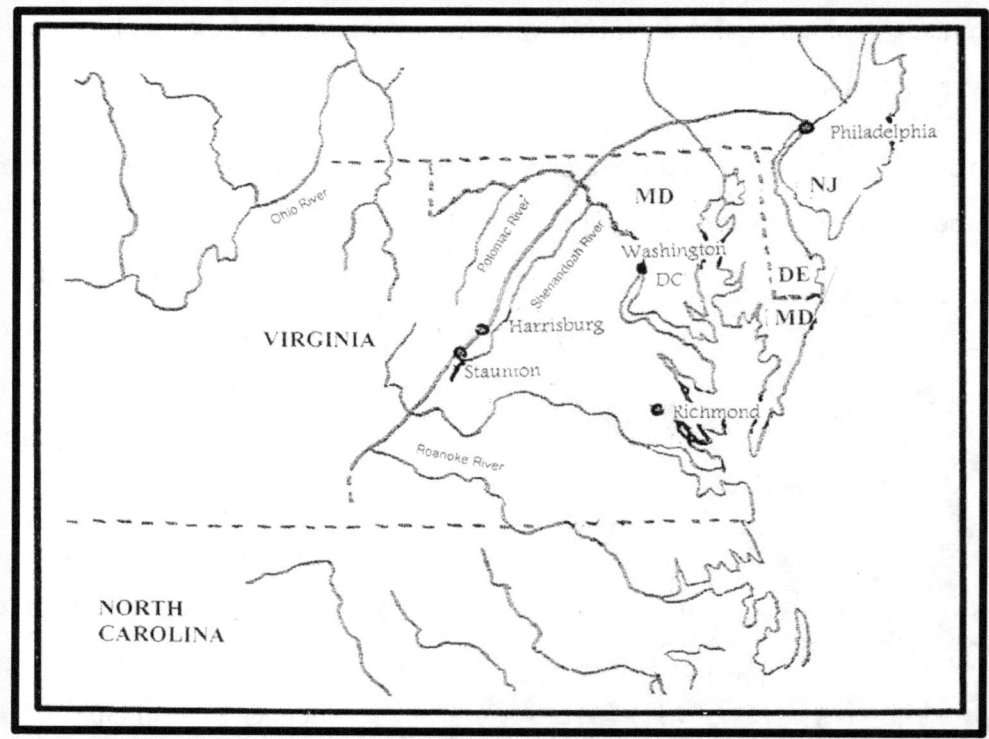

The Great Valley Road
Staunton is in Augusta County; Harrisburg is in Rockingham County

On July 26, 1848 Fountain (who was 6' tall, had a dark complexion, blue eyes, and dark hair,[4]) was married to Virginia Young in neighboring Augusta County. Virginia Young was born in Augusta County. Her grandparents, George and Catharine Young, had also moved down the Great Valley to Virginia from Pennsylvania about 1789. Virginia was the oldest of five siblings,

---

[2] Jacob's brother, Abraham, moved with his son, Thomas, to Kentucky, and Abraham Lincoln (later to become President) was born there in 1809.
[3] (Census, 1860)
[4] According to his military regimental enrollment form

3 brothers and 2 sisters. Virginia was able to read and write.[5] Her father, Jacob, died in 1846, just before she was married to Fountain at age 19.

Sometime between 1850 and 1855, Fountain and Virginia decided to move west. All of his family remained in Virginia, except for his brother Garland, who went to California about 1860. Fountain and Virginia left Rockingham County, Virginia with their four children, (twins John and Jake, James and Sis). Virginia's mother, Mariah, brother, George, and sisters, Hester and Cynthia, also moved with them.

From 1855-57 they were in Sangamon County, Illinois, where another daughter (Nealy), was born, and where one of Virginia's sisters, Cynthia, married Thomas Jefferson Dunlap. Abraham Lincoln was a practicing attorney in Sangamon, Illinois then and became more involved in politics during this time. Around the time Fountain May would have arrived in Illinois, Lincoln had a debate with Steven Douglas at the State Fair in Springfield. So it is possible that Fountain and his family would have been aware of, or even met, Lincoln.

In 1858 the family moved further west to Sullivan County, Missouri. Two more children were born here, Gus and William Garland. In the 1860 census, Fountain is shown as age 34; he owned $400 real estate[6] and $208 personal property. It appeared the family was thriving.

But the unrest in the nation was increasing. The Governor of Missouri had called for a vote on the issue of secession in February of 1861. Most Missourians were trying to remain neutral, but about a third of the people there wanted to secede. Then in April of 1861, the Civil War began, and Lincoln put out a call for soldiers. Missouri was expected to supply 4000 men. The Governor refused, saying it was illegal, abandoned the state capitol, and declared (illegally) that Missouri had seceded. But in spite of the Governor's efforts, various military companies began to organize. Recruiting for the 23rd Missouri, Fountain's future unit, began in July, 1861.

---

[5] (Census, 1860)
[6] Worth $10,800 in 2010

By then Fountain and his wife had seven children. Leaving them behind must have been difficult. But Fountain was from Virginia and had a grandfather who was a Patriot in the Revolutionary War. Virginia also had Patriots in her family. He may have not wanted his home state to secede and the Union to break apart. He may also have been a supporter of Lincoln. He was good friends with James T. Dunlap[7] who was organizing the company, so that may have influenced his decision. Although a farmer, Fountain no doubt had hunted as a boy in Virginia, and so was comfortable with firearms, and therefore felt qualified. Another incentive, especially since he was a farmer, was to obtain more land. Whatever his reason, apparently he felt strongly enough about the war, that when the call went out for soldiers, he enlisted.

---

[7] James' son married Virginia Young's sister while both families lived in Sangamon County, Illinois. Then all of them moved to Sullivan County, Missouri at about the same time.

MILITARY

Fountain Shelton May enrolled in the Union Army on Aug 17, 1861. His term was for three years. He was 35 yrs. old and had a wife and seven children. Some have asked "Why he would leave seven children to enroll in the war?" He must have felt strongly about the war. And leaving children behind on the farm was somewhat easier than it would seem to us now. Farmers had milk cows, chickens, and gardens. Farmers were more self reliant. Also Fountain had two sons who were 11 at the time he went to war. Certainly the boys, who were accustomed to helping around the farm, would be a great help to Virginia. And Virginia had her mother, sister, and brother close by to help her, as well.

It also may have been a way he could acquire more land. Blake Bell, historian at the Homestead National Monument said, "Civil War veterans were given special consideration under the Homestead Act, meaning that they were allowed to deduct their time of service off of the time that was required to prove up on their land. Homesteaders were required to live on their claim for five years and make improvements to the grounds. At the end of the five years, they received the land deed. Civil War veterans, however, had the incentive of deducting military service from the five year rule, being able to deduct up to four years of service toward receiving the deed." [8]

Fountain was enrolled by James T. Dunlap. He was mustered in Sept. 22, 1861 at Chillicothe, Missouri. About half the men were from Mercer County, but Company A of the 23rd Regiment of Missouri Volunteers (infantry) was organized at Wintersville, in Sullivan County, Missouri. James T. Dunlap, Fountain's old friend, was elected Captain and J.C. Webb and William Seaman became Lieutenants of the Company.

The Company was transported to Macon City, Missouri on October 15, 1861 and then back to Chillicothe, Missouri on November 1, 1861 where they spent the rest of the winter. During this first six months in the army they hadn't moved more than a few miles from home.

---

[8] (Dunker, 2011)

But things began to change in March, 1862. The Company, around 490 strong, was ordered to St. Louis and the 23rd Missouri was attached to Brig. Gen. Benjamin M. Prentiss' 6th Division. They were ordered south to join up with troops under Major General Ulysses S. Grant.

On April 1, 1862, loaded onto at least four steam riverboats, with new uniforms and rifles, they headed toward Pittsburg Landing. Grant was ordered to meet up with General Don Carlos Buell's Army from Ohio, for a battle near Corinth, in northern Mississippi. Grant's troops arrived before Buell's, since they were traveling by boat. There had been a lot of rain, which slowed supply wagons and Buell's troops. Grant's troops began arriving on the evening of the 4th and camped on a ridge overlooking the river. Others wouldn't arrive until shortly before sunrise on the 6th.

Tent Camp

There is some disagreement about when the 23rd Missouri arrived. Private John Peter Bagley, Company I, 23rd Missouri, wrote a poem, dated January 22, 1863 about the 23rd Missouri, in which he says "on the 5th at Pittsburg Landing we disembarked, Tindall commanding. And laid us down upon the ground. And there we slept all night quite sound"[9] This, written so soon after the event would seem to be the truth of when they arrived at Shiloh. The report of Lt. Col. Quin Morton to the Governor of Missouri, made Dec. 1, 1862 after his release from prison, states "At 7 A.M., I marched the regiment in the direction of General Prentiss' camp. After marching about 2 miles an officer of General Prentiss' staff ordered us to halt and prepare for action, which was promptly done." This report indicates that the 23rd Missouri was perhaps not in the camp that was surprised by the Confederates before breakfast that morning. But they certainly were present at the site. However, David W. Reed, also a veteran of the battle, and the first historian of Shiloh National Military Park, says "the 23rd Missouri arrived at the Landing Sunday morning, April 6, 1962. The 23rd Missouri reported to General Prentiss at his third position about 9:30 a.m. and was placed in line at once as part of his command."[10] As in any battle, I suppose, there will be conflicting reports. I will leave the reader to draw his/her own conclusions.

On April 2, the Confederate General Johnston received news that Buell's troops were progressing and making good time, and decided he had to make a move. He wanted to move on Grant's troops and beat him before Buell arrived. General Grant had no idea that an attack would be made on them there. He was preparing for a battle in Corinth and dismissed any idea that the Confederates were near.

Late in the day on April 4, just as the Union soldiers began to arrive, a cold rain began to fall, later coming down in torrents. This delayed the Confederates, who originally planned to attack earlier. But on the morning of the 5th, their troops were finally in place. The decision was made – the attack would take place on the 6th.

The Confederate soldiers had no idea they were so close to the Union front line. They sang songs, tested their rifles, yelled at each other. The officers rushed around quieting them, certain that the Union soldiers must have heard them. But, amazingly, there was no effect on the Union troops. Their camps had been made haphazardly when they arrived, since they did not expect to fight there. Brigadier General William Tecumseh Sherman was camped near the Shiloh Church,

---

[9] (Crumpacker, 1977, p. 456)
[10] (Reed, 1903, p. 58)

which gave the battle its name. Union troops were scattered widely throughout the area, and they assumed that the soldiers they heard were other Union troops.

Shiloh Meeting House

April 6 arrived - bright and warm. The Union soldiers were scheduled to have a day of rest. Breakfast was prepared. The privates played cards, smoked and drank and generally relaxed. Only one officer was suspicious. Colonel Jesse Appler saw some men moving across a ridge about a mile away and sent out a detachment of men to investigate. The group ran into the lead soldiers of the Confederate detachment and exchanged a few shots. They reported this to Colonel Appler who immediately rode to Sherman's headquarters and reported that the Confederates were less than a mile from his line. Sherman did not believe him and exclaimed angrily, "Take your damned regiment back to Ohio! Beauregard is not such a fool as to leave his base of operations and attack us in ours. There is no enemy nearer than Corinth!"[11] In reality the Confederates were only a few hundred yards away.

Fountain May and the 23rd Missouri Infantry were in the middle of it all with Prentiss' 6th Regiment

---

[11] (Foote, 1998, p. 198)

Grant's headquarters boat during the Shiloh campaign was the Tigress, second from left.

Grant's headquarters at Pittsburg Landing

Grant did not receive any of the reports about Confederates being near. He was at his headquarters in Savannah nine miles away from Pittsburg Landing. He had told his commanders to wait for Buell's army. Many of them, including General Prentiss, understood this to mean that confrontation should be avoided. But by 3:00 AM on the morning of the 6th, there was too much activity to ignore. One of Prentiss's officers, Colonel Everett Peabody, sent a message to Prentiss that he believed Confederates were on the front lines. He got no reply. Believing it to be in the best interest of everyone, he sent out a scouting party. They surprised a Confederate unit and opened fire. The Confederates retreated. As they made their way through some brush in pursuit, the first man in the Battle of Shiloh was killed – Lt. Frederick Klinger.

Colonel Peabody heard the shooting and ordered 300 men forward. These men were still engaged with the small attachment of Confederate troops when the first wave of the full Confederate Army swarmed over the ridge and through the trees. Suddenly the Union men in the main camps saw friends and soldiers bursting through the trees, screaming that the entire Confederate Army was coming. Within fifteen minutes, 30 men and 48 horses had been killed.

Prentiss accused Peabody of provoking the attack. Peabody responded icily that he was always responsible for his actions, mounted his horse and rode into battle. Soon he would be dead - he was killed in battle within a few hours.

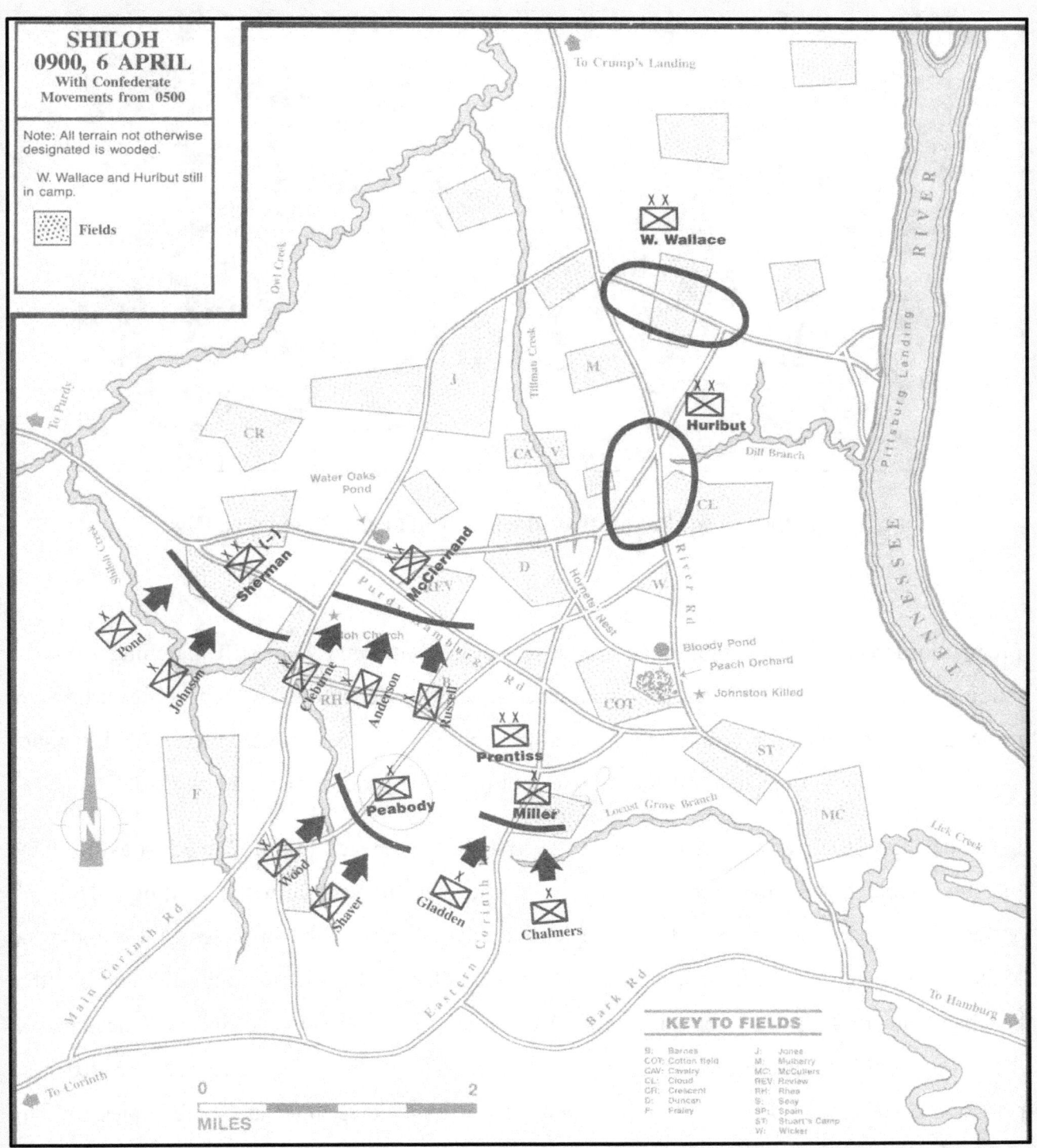

Troops fleeing to the safety of the bluffs near the Tennessee River

Prentiss ordered every available man to the front line, but some were still marching from the landing, including the 23rd Missouri. As they marched, they encountered men in blue who were running for their lives through the timber and back into camp. Some were bloody with wounds and most yelled warnings of what was ahead. But the 23rd Missouri marched onward.

In the center of the Union line, Prentiss watched as his line began to crumble. Just as it looked like the whole line would crumble, the rest of the men arrived from the landing. The 23rd Missouri arrived just before 9:00 and took their place between the brigades of Peabody and Miller. They began defending what it now known as "the sunken road" – an old farm road that had been cut through heavy brush. Under continuous fire, they held the line, but the flank on their right was collapsing, with troops from other units fleeing to safety. The eroded road provided a shallow trench in which they could take shelter and shoot at Confederates running across the field.

Around 10:00, the Confederates who had overrun Sherman's camp, stopped to eat the Union breakfasts that had been hastily left behind. Many of them hadn't eaten in over 24 hours. Prentiss took advantage of this break in the action to gather his scattered troops and regroup.

The area around "the sunken road" was now manned with at least 6,000 men and several cannons. They were tired, battered and bloody, but they were holding the line.

At 12:30 the Confederates attacked the center of the Union line (mostly the 23rd Missouri) at "the sunken road" - cannon balls were flying, shells were exploding, bullets whizzing by, bark flying off trees. The Confederates said it sounded like a swarm of bees and soon "the sunken road" was known by a new name – "The Hornet's Nest".

The Hornet's Nest by Thomas Corwin Lindsay

By 2:30 in the afternoon, the 23rd was holding their line quite well. But the lines on either side were collapsing. Thousands of men poured out of the forest in retreat toward the river. If this continued, soon the entire Union force would be pinned against the river. At 3:00 there were more men on the river bank than there were fighting on the lines. Grant rode over and found Prentiss at The Hornet's Nest and advised him of the situation. Grant ordered Prentiss to hold his position at all costs. This would allow the rest of the army to escape across the river. Prentiss's 6th Division would be sacrificed. At the beginning of the day, Prentiss had over 5,000 men. Hundreds were already dead and many others had been wounded. Only about 2,000 remained to hold off the Confederates. Initially, the 23rd Missouri had been on the far left end of Prentiss' line. But by 5:15, they were getting fire not only from the front, but from the left, right, and rear. They were surrounded! Around 5:30, after fighting for eight hours, Prentiss saw that there was no way out, and ordered them to surrender. Half the men of the regiment were now prisoners of the Confederates. Fountain Shelton May was one of them. But they accomplished a great feat – holding off the Confederates long enough for the rest of the army to escape.

"Prentiss had lost his (division) by standing fast; lost men, guns, colors, and finally the position itself: lost all, in fact, but honor. Yet he had saved far more in saving that. Sherman and McClernand had saved their divisions by retreating, but Prentiss had saved Grant by standing fast."[12]

That evening, while Fountain May sat prisoner in the enemy's camp, the Union Army re-grouped and readied for another day of battle. Both sides took the evening to rest. It was starting to rain and all of them were weary. But thousands of General Buell's troops arrived during the night. And the next morning, when the battle resumed, the Union had the upper hand. The Union had fresh troops and lots of them. And so, by afternoon, the Confederates, outnumbered and overwhelmed, withdrew.

---

[12] (Foote, 1998, p. 210)

PRISONER OF WAR

On the evening of April 6, 1862, Fountain May must have felt that he had seen the most terrible horror, but the worst was yet to come.

After the prisoners were taken, they were marched about 5 miles away from the battlefield. They bedded down, as best they could, in a corn field, with guards around them. If that wasn't bad enough, it began to rain in torrents. They had no blankets, but they were allowed to get some wood to make a fire, which helped some.

The next morning, guards counted 2200-2500 prisoners, including many officers and General Prentiss. Prisoners were given a small piece of raw pork about the size of two fingers, and some moldy crackers. Then they hastily got ready to leave for Corinth, about 15 miles away. The message had been delivered that Grant was pushing back the Confederates, so they felt the Union was on their tail.

The rains had made the roads nearly impassable - in some places the water was knee deep. Finally, just before dark, they reached Corinth, lying down on the ground to rest at last. Shortly though, the guards began loading them onto railroad cars, which took until almost midnight. If that wasn't bad enough, it was raining again.

The railroad cars were old and some were covered with manure from animals. There was no straw or place to sit to avoid it. So off they went, sitting in filth, for the next 18 hours, on the way to Memphis. As they passed the various towns, large crowds would gather to see the Yankee prisoners. They reached Memphis just before dark. There the officers were separated from the soldiers and were taken to different buildings. They were never reunited during their imprisonment. It was raining again – and there was nothing to eat.

The soldiers were placed in a large 3-story building, but were not given any bedding or blankets. Around midnight they were given some more pork, partially cooked, and some crackers. It had been two days and nights without a real meal. The raw pork made some soldiers sick, but this was what they were given during the entire time they remained in Memphis. A few soldiers, who had money, were able to buy some bread from boys who brought it to sell. But many developed diarrhea. The guards were generally as kind as they could be, under the circumstances; they were mostly home folk, serving as guards. The prisoners remained in Memphis until Sunday evening, the 13th of April. It had been a terrible week.

On Sunday, they were moved to Mobile, Alabama. A few soldiers were sent off to different places. The railroad cars, this time, were much cleaner. And the weather was also better. Once again, large crowds came out at every station to gaze at the sight. In Canton, Mississippi, an especially large, insulting crowd showed up. But in Jackson, a small child was heard to say "Why, these ain't Yankees, they look just like we do!"[13]

At Mobile, the prisoners were taken to some old cotton sheds. The opening between the buildings was closed up with boards to make a pen between the buildings, and there was no shade, so it was very hot. There was nothing to lie on but the bare wooden floor. In a few days, all the men had blisters on any skin that wasn't covered. Here they were given some hard bread and a little poor-quality corned beef. Sometimes, because it was so hot, the meat was spoiled before they got it. The meat was brought in quarters, so they had to divide it as fairly as they could without any utensils. They also brought corn meal in sacks and barrels, which had to be divided up in the same way. They were given skillets and pans to cook with, and a few plates, knives and forks. The yard quickly became filthy and had a disagreeable smell. The guards here spoke French, and were as kind as they were allowed to be, but they appeared to be terrified of the Confederate officers.

---

[13] (Kiner, 1863, p. 76)

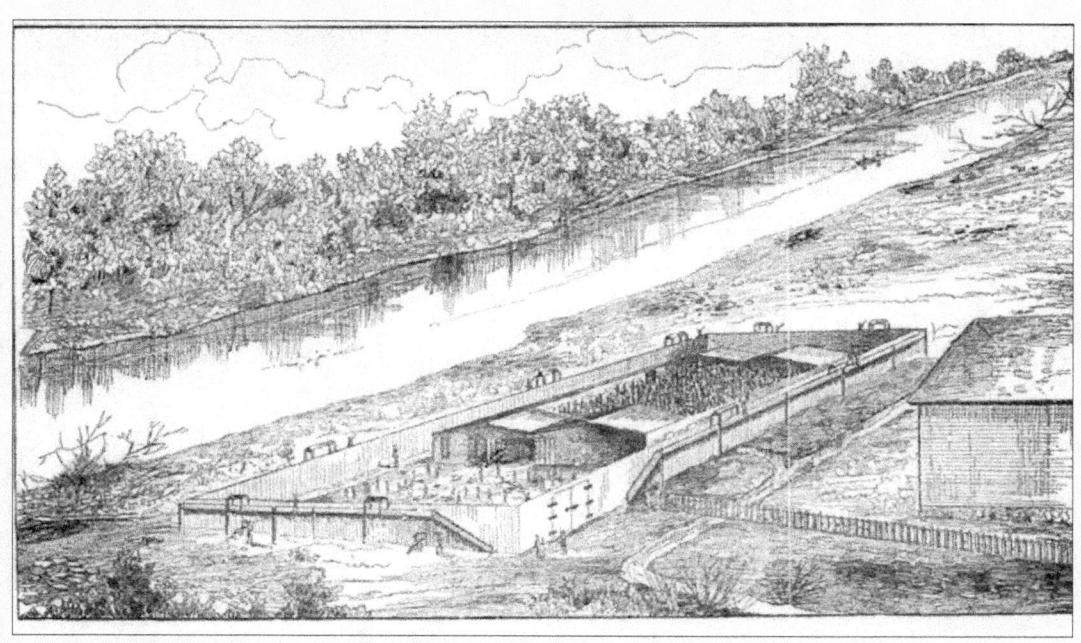

Cahaba Prison at Catawba, Alabama

After almost a week, on the 19th of April, the prisoners were moved to Cahawba, Alabama, aboard a steamer. This time they were separated according to their origin state, with Iowa being moved first. In Cahaba, their quarters were in a new brick warehouse, not completely finished and only partly covered. There was no outlet for smoke and even bathroom duties had to be carried out inside the building. Soon the stench became horrible. The food was the worst here of any they'd had. The meat was always spoiled. Sometimes, even though the men were hungry, they simply refused to eat it. The bread was made of corn meal and flour, which they had to bake themselves. A few of the prisoners died. Despite the conditions, however, Cahaba Prison was the least deadly of the war's military prisons.

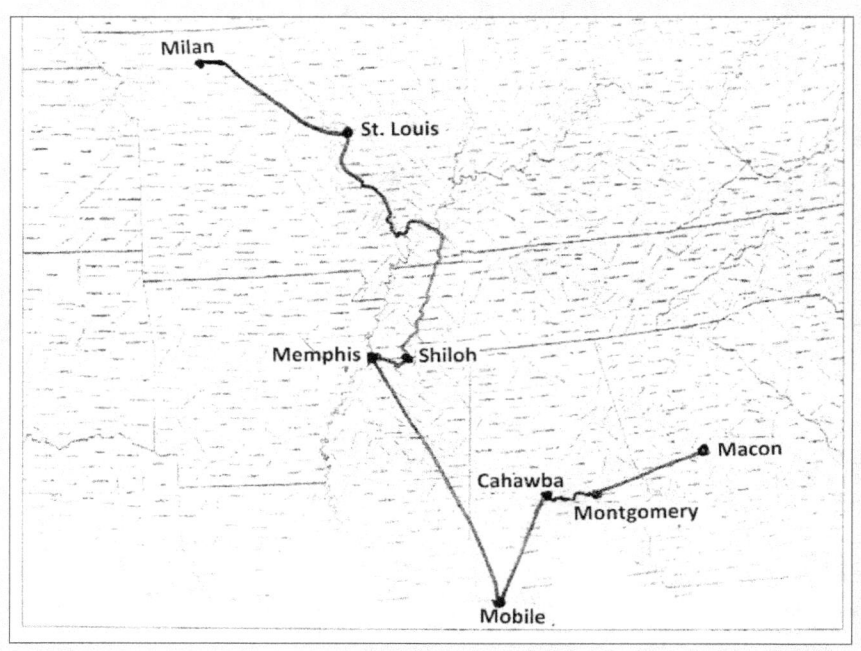

Fountain May's route from Milan, Missouri to Macon, Georgia

On the 2nd of May the prisoners were moved to Montgomery, Alabama aboard another steamer ship. It took only one day and when they arrived they were taken to the fairgrounds and housed in the amphitheater for the night. With little to eat, the next morning they left for Macon, Georgia, this time in railroad freight cars, arriving around noon the next day. It was the 4th of May. They had arrived at Camp Oglethorpe.

By this time, the men were very weak. Having had little nourishment for nearly a month, and most of that spoiled, plus the punishing environments that they'd had to endure, they were sick, tired, and vulnerable.

The City of Macon did not want the prisoners. They had tried to discourage officials from sending prisoners to them. They already had several hospitals in town for wounded Confederate soldiers and were having trouble feeding the civilian population. They did not know how they would feed the Union prisoners. But officials persisted and the prisoners began to arrive – 800 in early May.

Camp Oglethorpe was on the fairgrounds. It was about 15-20 acres total size, enclosed by a picket fence. In the northwest corner there was a grove of pine trees. Near the grove there were 3 large frame buildings and 2 smaller frame buildings. One of the smaller frame buildings was used for a shop for the doctors; the other was a cook house for the hospital. The best of the large buildings was used as a hospital. There was a running spring in the camp, but the water was not

Camp Oglethorpe
A Sketch of prisoners receiving rations

of very good quality. There was also a well. This was the first time in almost a month that the prisoners were able to wash themselves and their clothes. Many were already sick, or soon became sick. Twenty men died during May. Another 636 men arrived May 31.

The first two months went pretty well. The food was reasonably good. Each day the men were given one pound of flour or meal; ¾ pound of pork; some rice; some sugar or molasses; rye, which was used for coffee. They even had a small portion of soap. They had freedom to exercise, so they began walking and playing ball. Exercise helped their health, and also took their minds of their predicament.

Confederate Major Hardee was in charge of the prison until May 20. He was considered fair and kind. When he was transferred, however, Major J. E. Rylander took over. He was "cruel, tyrannical, presumptuous, overbearing, and hated"[14] The guards were mostly kind and showed sympathy. Often they could not read or write the names of those they were guarding, even to call the roll. Most just wanted peace, but some were rebellious and cruel. Staking was a practice done for punishment of the prisoners. The man would be staked face-down to the ground, his hands, legs and neck secured with forked sticks, and left for hours at a time.

On the 22nd of June, orders were received to parole all the privates who had been at Shiloh. Officers were to be retained. So on the 24th, the prisoners were lined up and given an oath not to take up arms until they were exchanged. Then they left for Atlanta and Chattanooga to join Union forces in Gen. Mitchell's command. There were, for some reason, about 500 who were rejected, kept at Montgomery, Alabama, and sent back to prison at Oglethorpe. Fountain May was one of these. Imagine the disappointment! It is not known why they were rejected. Apparently there was some order to Gen. Mitchell that gave him this authority.

Back at Oglethorpe, the guards then took some of the cooking utensils from the camp, leaving only those utensils necessary for the 100 men who were remaining. More prisoners kept arriving all summer until there were 1200-1400 present. There were prisoners from almost every state in the North and 140 different regiments. Even after the number of men increased to 1400, they still had this small amount of cooking equipment. Conditions became worse. The nights were cold and there were no blankets. Flour was changed to rice or corn meal. The corn meal was very coarse, often with pieces of cob in it. The men gathered up any pieces of iron or tin that could be found, to use for pans or plates.

"You could see men baking at almost all hours of the day or night; this was because of the scarcity of things to bake in. It really looked pitiable to see hungry men, young and old, holding an old piece of tin or iron over a smoking fire, with a batch of coarse corn dough upon it, trying to bake it, and perhaps when done, it was so sad, or burnt and smoked, that it was not fit for a dog to eat. But what could we do? We had no better. For plates we used any old scrap of tin we could find, while some made them out of a pine board or shingle. A few of us, however, had good tin plates. As for knives and forks the fingers answered all purposes. The bread however was the best part of our living compared to the meat. They would call us all into line and give us

---
[14] (Kiner, 1863, p. 121)

printed tickets good for seven day's rations, which were gathered up by our quartermaster, who drew rations for the number of tickets; these they hauled into the yard under the trees. The meal was brought in barrels, or old sugar hogsheads; the meat was thrown out upon the ground and literally crawled with maggots. They put guards around these rations until they were issued, and we often told them it was necessary to guard it to keep it from crawling off. Some of these hams and sides of meat were so badly spoiled that we could push a finger through and through them, as if they were mince meat. In fact, that was what was the matter with it, the worms had minced it too much. It had spoiled mostly from want of salt, for the grease we got from it was not salt enough to use for gravy. Of this rotten stuff, we got one half pound to the man per day. The maggots upon it were of the largest kind; perhaps I should call them skippers, for they could skip about and jump several feet at one leap; from their size I judged the climate agreed with them. There was, however, a kind much smaller, which worked into the meat, though it looked middling good, similar to those in cheese, and we could not see them until the meat was cooked, when they made their appearance on the top of the water in the pot, and floated around like clever sized grains of rice."[15]

Some of the men, although they were practically starving, refused to eat the meat. Others mixed in corn meal, so the maggots could not be seen, and ate it anyway. Not all the meat was in this condition, but about a third of it was. And due to the sparse amount given to them to begin with, this had to be hard to bear.

Late in the summer the men began to sell their meat to the local citizens. Amazingly, they were anxious to get it, because food was scarce for them also. With this money from selling the meat, they bought yams, sweet potatoes, tomatoes, or any vegetables or fruits they could get. Only sweet potatoes were plentiful. But after they began to do this, the prisoners did much better.

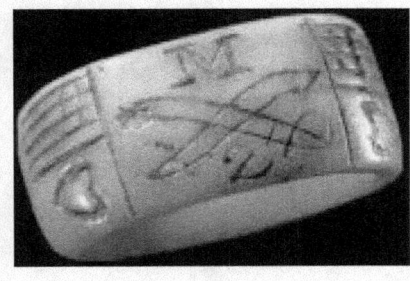
With the bones in the meat, some men began to carve jewelry – rings, pins, and other items. Not only did it keep them busy, but they were able to sell this jewelry to local residents and then buy additional vegetables. Rings would bring about 25 cents to $1.00. Flour was $40 a barrel; white potatoes were $8 a barrel.

---

[15] (Kiner, 1863, p. 104)

The prisoner's clothes were becoming very tattered and worn. They would wash them in the stream, hang them on the fence to dry and lie in the stream until they were dry again. There were few blankets and because they were sleeping outside on the ground, many began to get sick.

This was compounded by the diarrhea they had. With no body fat, they would shiver through the nights. Even the men who were in the hospital had to lie on the floor. There were 2 doctors in the hospital and they did the best they could with little or no medicines or supplies. Sometimes local citizens would bring mattresses or pieces of clothing. Each day, some of the prisoners would serve as nurses. It was unpleasant duty and most avoided it, not wanting to see their own in such bad conditions.

"Towards the latter part of the summer the mortality among us became great, and with few exceptions we had every day from one to seven of our men to bury. I have known them to get so poor that their thighs were no larger than a man's arms, and they were really nothing more than living skeletons, yet they would try to keep about until in many cases they would drop dead from their feet. Others would die sitting against a tree, or anywhere, while many would die so easily upon their beds, without a groan or a sigh, that even the nurses were not aware of it."[16]

---

[16] (Kiner, 1863, p. 113)

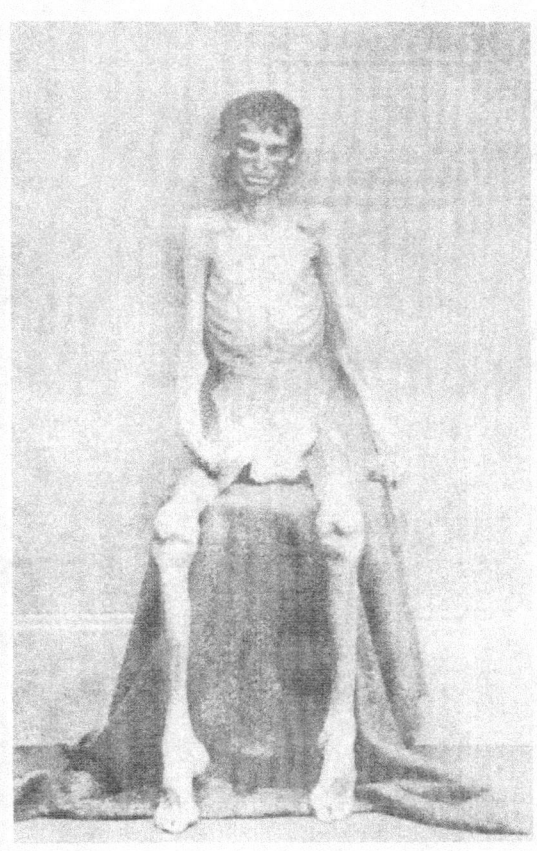

A Union soldier who survived

Out of the thousands of prisoners taken at Shiloh, about 200 died at Camp Oglethorpe.

After June of 1862, the prisoners were buried on a ridge southwest of the camp. Between 1865 and 1868 the bodies of burials at Camp Oglethorpe were moved and reburied in the Andersonville National Cemetery. They are buried there in Section B. "As part of the effort between 1865 and 1870 to rebury battlefield casualties, 70 national cemeteries were opened and 300,000 remains gathered and reburied. Of the total buried, 142,000 were unknown."[17]

Fountain Shelton May died September 5, 1862. He must have suffered a wound to his leg. Some of his records state that he died from "a corroborated leg and chronic diarrhea." It is not known if his grave was one of the ones relocated. During the summer of 1862 when the camp was under the control of Major J. E. Rylander, the dead were often denied burial for days or sometimes not buried at all. No record of his burial has yet been found.

---

[17] (Affairs)

Andersonville National Cemetery
Andersonville, Georgia

THE NOBLE TWENTY THIRD
By Peter Bagley

Parole Prisoner, Company I, 23rd Missouri Volunteers
Osage City, Missouri
January 22, 1863

"The following poem was written in honor of the Twenty-Third, which was largely made up of Sullivan County men. The spelling and punctuation is exactly as written on the original. It vividly describes the hardships endured by the brave men. Being held in a prison camp was almost worse than death. No toilet facilities were readily available. Dysentery, flies, lack of shelter, blankets, inadequate water supply, which was often contaminated from the latrines. One prisoner personally stated the men picked the undigested grains of corn from the horse and mule dung, which was dropped when the animals hauled supplies into the camp, and ate the grains to avert starvation as long as possible. Teeth fell out, sores covered their bodies, and health failed. So many died they were hauled from the stockade by wagons. Such is the price for liberty."[18]

Note: The poem can also be found on page 455 of the History of Sullivan County Missouri.

---

[18] (Crumpacker, 1977, p. 455)

"THE NOBLE TWENTY THIRD"
Tune: Duane Street (or Hail, Sovereign Love)

Attention give both far and near
A truthful story you shal hear
And I speak I pledge my word
Its of the noble Twenty Third

And as we marched along each street
The fifes did play and drums did beat
And flags were waved and shouts were heard
In honor of the Twenty Third

We marched along the (?) boat
Oer which the stars and stripes did float
And from the cheers we might infered
That much depend pon the Twenty Third

And on the 5th at Pittsburg Landing
We disembarked, Tindall Commanding
And laid us down upon the ground
And there we slept all night quite sound

Early next morning, breakfast oer
We heard the thundering cannons roar
Our knapsacks slung we started out
To ascertan what twas bout

We met the wounded by the score
Some mourned and groaned while others swore
They said that if we went ahead
Wed soon be number with the dead

But onward, onward was our motto
Until the little field we got to
And there we formed a line of battle
Mid cannons roar and muskets rattle

The shot and shell came whizzing-by
As we behind the fence did lie
Intending if the rebs did come
To send them to their final home

An aid came dashing up and said
The Twenty Third must go ahead
Redeem the camp that had been lost
No matter what might be the cost

Brave Tindall with his sword in hand
Raised his stirups and gave command
At quick step forward we did rush
And met the rebels in the brush

The leaden hail flew thick and fast
A scattered death at every blast
Yet nothing daunted or dismayed
Our muskets manfully we played

The rabid rebels fierce for blood
Came rushing on us like a flood
But ah the noble Twenty Third
Firm as gibraltar never stirred

We drove them back time and again
And many were the rebels slain
At length by thousands al around
Our selves completely bagged we found

About this time brave Tindall fell
And many more we loved so well
But worse than all the stripes and stars
Lay furled beneath the stars and bars

Although we of our arms were stripped
We felt that we could not be whipped
And hoped that we might have the luck
With equal numbers to try our pluck

For months in Dixie we did stay
And on the ground we had to lay
Without a blanket or a bed
While our forms the vermin fed

With musty bread and beef as bad
We very little of it had
Our house we used without a broom
For kitchen, priva, dining room

But thank the Lord weer now exchanged
And though our ranks are some deranged
This matter we will soon set right
And then we're ready for a fight

And if we ever have a chance
We'll either die or els advance
And pay them for their beef and bread
With bayonets and cone shaped lead

Come fellow soldiers to your post
Prepare to meet the rebel host
Together all with one accord
And hast to join the Twenty Third

In January sixty three
This was composed for you and me
It has once more our memory stirred
In honor of the Twenty Third

MILITARY RECORDS

M | 23 | Mo.

Fountain May

_____, Co. F, 23 Reg't Missouri Inf.

Appears on

Regimental Descriptive Book

of the regiment named above.

DESCRIPTION.

Age 34 years; height 6 feet __ inches.
Complexion Dark
Eyes Blue; hair Dark
Where born Rockingham Va
Occupation Farmer

ENLISTMENT.

When Aug 17, 186_.
Where Sullivan Co
By whom J. C. Dunlap; term 3 y'rs.
Remarks: Died

MEMORANDUM FROM PRISONER OF WAR RECORDS.   No. _____

(This blank to be used only in the arrangement of said records.)

NAME	RANK	ORGANIZATION				INFORMATION OBTAINED FROM—			
		No. of Reg't	State	Arm of Service	Co.	Records of—	Vol.	Page.	Vol.	Page.
						DVB	1	218		
May Fountain	P.	93	Mo.		E.	Ex	1	258		

7.

Captured at _Shiloh Tenn Apl 6_, 186 2, confined at Richmond, Va., _____, 186 ,
Pris. of war at Montgomery, Ala. May 24, 1862.
Admitted to Hospital at _____
where he died at Macon Ga Sept 21, 186 2, of Corroborated by O.R. Med. Direct C.S.A. 1773-B.77
Paroled at _____, 186 ; reported at Camp Parole, Md., _____, 186 .

Copied by B.V.E.
See Axam No 39. 12. Iowa J.S. 3.11.75

WIDOW'S PENSION

"All volunteers entering the service with their organizations after the breaking out of the war and up to Dec. 23d, 1863, inclusive, are entitled to $100. All the above are paid to the heirs of deceased soldiers in the order named, namely, to widow, children, father, mother, brothers and sisters. All who have been confined in rebel prisons are entitled to 25 cents per day for each day if they have not drawn such commutation. Heirs of Prisoners of War are entitled to commutation for rations at twenty-five cents per pay, for the time the soldier was held prisoner. The heirs are, first the widow, if she has not re-married, next the children, next the parents, and if neither of these are living, then the brothers and sisters." [19] (An Act to Grant Pensions, July 1862)

Virginia May applied for a widow's pension on November 28, 1862. The records do not indicate if she received the $100 payment for volunteers, or the 25 cents per day for the time he spent in prison. But the regulations allowed for those payments, so she probably did receive them. Fountain was in prison for 152 days, so she would have received $38 for that time.

Capt. James T. Dunlap, who enrolled Fountain initially, was also a prisoner at Macon, Georgia, when Fountain died. But he was an officer, so he was separated from the volunteers. Capt. Dunlap was released in October and returned home. And in November, he gave a sworn statement to assist Virginia May in filing for a widow's pension.

Virginia received notice that her application had been received on January 7, 1863, and received notice that she would receive $8 per month[20] beginning September 5, 1862, the date that Fountain died. On March 5, 1869, under The Act of July 25, 1866, Virginia filed a claim for Increase of Pension. This act gave the children of veterans $2 per month. So Virginia received $8 per month as a widow and $2 per month for four children who were under the age of sixteen in 1866.[21] On May 26, 1869 she received notice that her claim was approved. She probably received about $360 in arrears as the Act was effective July 25, 1866. On March 9, 1886, Congress approved an increase for widows to $12 per month. Virginia received this pension until she died in on July 19, 1900.

---

[19] (The Valley of the Shadow)
[20] Worth $143 in 2010
[21] Worth $255 in 2010

Virginia May was faced with the difficult task of raising seven children without their father. She was fortunate to have much family around her to help. And there were uncles who, I am sure, stood in Fountain's place. Apparently she did a magnificent job. All her children were successful, productive citizens. All but one – the youngest, William Garland -- remained in Missouri throughout their lives. He chose to go west to Kansas, where he homesteaded in Stevens County. Emma (or "Sis" as she was called) was devoted to her mother, often residing with her, up until her death in 1900. Even though Fountain, paid the ultimate price, Virginia was able to continue on and lived a full life without him at her side.

ARMY PENSION.
Widow's Claim.

State of Missouri
County of Sullivan } ss.

On this 28th day of November A.D. one thousand eight hundred and sixty two personally appeared, before me, Clark H. T. McClanahan Clerk of the Circuit Court of Sullivan Co, Mo (1) Virginia May a resident of Milan in Sullivan County, State of Missouri aged 34 years, who being first duly sworn according to law, doth on her oath make the following declaration in order to obtain the benefit of the provisions made by the Act of Congress approved July 24th, 1862. That she is the widow of Fountain May late of Sullivan County, State of Missouri who was a (2) private in Company (4) "A" commanded by Capt. J. T. Tindall in the 23rd Regiment of Missouri Volunteers commanded by Col. J. T. Tindall (in the war of 1861) who died on the fifth day of September 1862 at Macon in County, State of Georgia that his death was caused by disease contracted while in the service of the United States—for proof of which she would respectfully refer you to the muster or pay rolls of said Company

She further declares that she was married to the said (2) Fountain May on the 26 day of May 1848 at Stanton in Augusta County, State of Virginia by Daniel W. Arnold a Preacher and that her name before marriage was Virginia Young. She further states that she believes there is a public record of her said marriage, and there is no private or family record, and that the best evidence she is able to procure of her said marriage, is (5) the affidavits of two witnesses who were present at the time of the solemnization of the marriage from the fact that there is no communication by mail from this place to Stanton Augusta Co. Va. That her husband, the aforesaid (2) Fountain May died on the day above mentioned, and that she has remained a widow ever since that period, as will appear by reference to the proof hereto annexed. She also declares that she had by her said husband 7 children, the names, ages, and residence of whom under sixteen years of age at the decease of her said husband, is as follows: Jacob H. May John E. May are both 12 years old Emily E. May aged ten years James L May aged eight years Cornelia J May six years Samuel A May aged four years old and Wm G May aged two

33

H. T. McClenahan
S. H. & B. Cochrane } (6) Virginia May (seal)

Also, personally appeared Capt. J. T. Dunlap a resident of Milan in Sullivan County, State of Missouri, and Mariah Young a resident of Milan in Sullivan County, State of Missouri, persons whom I certify to be respectable and entitled to credit, and who being, by me, first duly sworn, say they were present and saw Mrs. (1) Virginia May her name, to the foregoing declaration, and they further swear that they have been personally acquainted with the said (1) Virginia May and her husband (2) Fountain May who was a (3) private in Company (4) "A," commanded by Capt. J. T. Dunlap in the 23rd Regiment of Missouri Volunteers commanded by Col. J. T. Tindall in the war of 1861, for upwards of 17 years, and know that they lived together as man and wife, and were so reputed, and never heard the same doubted. That (5) they were present at the wedding and saw them married &

they know that the said (1) Virginia May was married to the aforesaid soldier at Stanton in Augusta County, State of Virginia on the 26' day of May 1848, by David W. Arnold a ____, and that her name before marriage was Virginia Young. That from the personal knowledge of Capt. J. T. Dunlap one of the witnesses who served with him they know that the said soldier died at Macon in ____ County, State of Georgia, on or about the 5" day of September 1862, while in the service of the United States; and that the said (1) Virginia May has remained a widow ever since that period; also, that the said soldier left the following child-ren under 16 years of age at the time of his decease, whose names, age and residence is as follows: Jacob H. May, John E. May twins, aged twelve years, Emily C. May aged ten years, James S. May aged eight years, Fountain J. May aged six years, Samuel A. May aged four years, & M. J. May aged two years all of whom reside with their mother in Sullivan County Mo.

They further declare that the claimant has not in any way been engaged in, or aided, or abetted the rebellion in the United States—that their knowledge of the identity of her husband with the soldier, is derived from (7) James T. Dunlap a witness here who served with him & from seeing him frequently while in the service

They further declare that they have no interest in this claim, in any way whatever, and do reside as above stated.

(S) James D. Dunlap
(S) Maria Young

Sworn to and subscribed before me, on this 28th day of November 1862, and I certify that I have no interest, direct or indirect, in the prosecution of this claim. In witness whereof I have hereunto set my hand & affixed my official seal.

H. T. McClanahan, Clerk

State of Missouri,
County of Sullivan, SS.

I, H. T. McClanahan, Clerk of the Circuit Court within and for the County and State aforesaid, do hereby certify that on this the 28th day of November 1862, appeared Virginia May who is personally known to me to be the same person whose name is subscribed to the foregoing Power of Attorney as a party thereto, and acknowledged the same to be her act and deed, for the purposes therein mentioned.

In testimony whereof I have hereunto subscribed my name and affixed my official seal.

H. T. McClanahan, Clerk

INSTRUCTIONS.

1. Claimant's name.
2. Soldier's name.
3. Soldier's rank.
4. Alphabetical title of Company

No. 2167

Missouri

Virginia May

widow of Fountain May
Rank Private
Company A
Regiment 23d Missouri Vols.

St. ~~Louis~~ Mo. Agency.
Rate per month, $8
Commencing 5th Sept. 1862.

Certificate dated 18, May 1863,
and sent to Aaron D. Burgess
Milan,
Missouri

Act 14th July, 1862.

Book A. Vol. 1. Page 270.
Chipman, Hosmer & Co.
Present

No. 2167

Holloped

Virginia Mary

WIDOW OF

Townsend Mary

Rank *Pvt* Co. *K*
Regt. *23 Wis Vols*

Missouri City Agency.

Rate per Month. $8

Commencing 1 Sept 1862

Additional sum of $2 per Month for each of the following children, until arriving at the age of 16 years, commencing 23 July 1866

James S. 11 Aug 1810
Cornelia J. 3 Oct 1872
Samuel H. 11 Sept 1874
William G. 10 June 1876

DEAD.

Certificate dated 26 May 1867
Sent to *Chipman Hosmer & Co*
Present

Act 14th July, 1862.
Book C Vol. 17 Page 124
J. W. Davis Clerk

Stamped Dead after Virginia's death

Virginia May's gravesite at Glaze Cemetery, Sullivan County, Missouri

This memorial stone stands in front of the Sullivan County Court House in Milan, Missouri

LIST OF SOLDIERS

FROM SULLIVAN COUNTY

IN THE 23rd MISSOURI INFANTRY

Company A

The following list of soldiers from Sullivan County in the 23rd Missouri Infantry, Company A should not be considered complete and may have inaccuracies. It was assembled from a variety of resources and is not original research on my part. Every effort was made to be accurate, but due to the number of men involved, time would not allow research on each one. I regret any omissions or inaccuracies.

***** - on memorial stone at Sullivan County Courthouse

ALLEN, George W.; Company A; Rank in: Pvt; Rank out: Cpl; Born about 1847 in Missouri; Listed in the 1860 Census of Sullivan County with mother, Sarah Allen.

BASKETT, George P.; Companies I & A; Rank in: Pvt; 15 years old; Rank out: Pvt; Born Oct 20, 1845 in Milan, Missouri, Son of Stephen & Mary Baskett; Listed in the 1860 Census of Sullivan County; Married Mary Fields on June 29, 1865 in Linn County, Missouri; Resided in Linn and Sullivan Counties, Missouri; Died March 19, 1888; Buried at Morris Chapel Cemetery, Linn County, Missouri.

BRUNER, Henry C.; Company A; Rank in: Pvt, 19 years old; Rank out: Pvt; Born in 1843 in Pennsylvania; Son of Henry and Isabella Bruner; Married Martha Nowels; Listed in the 1880 Census of Polk Township, Sullivan County, Missouri; Lived in Green City, Sullivan, Missouri; Henry Bruner applied for a pension on July 5, 1876.

BUSICK, Dennis S.; Company A; Rank in: Pvt; Rank out: Pvt; Born 1841 in North Carolina; Son of Caleb Busick; Listed in the 1860 Census of Sullivan County, Missouri (West Locust); Lived in Judson, Sullivan County, Missouri; Applied for a pension in 1866 in Missouri.

BUSICK, Sample C.; Company A; Rank in: Pvt, 21 years old; Rank out: Pvt; Born 1840 in North Carolina; son of Andrew and Arrilla Busick; Listed in the 1860 Census of Sullivan County, Missouri (West Locust).

COCHRAN, Robert; Company A; Rank in: Pvt; Rank out: Pvt; Born 1841 in Pennsylvania; Son of Robert & Jame Cochrane; Listed in 1860 census of Sullivan County, Missouri; Lived in Milan.

COOPMAN, James M.; Company A; Rank in: Sgt; Rank out: Sgt; Born 1834 in Indiana; Married Catharine; Listed in the 1860 Census of Sullivan County, Missouri, as a farmer.

COUCH, Joseph Henry; Companies A & G; Rank in: Pvt, 19 years old; Rank out: Pvt; Born 1842 in Sullivan County, Missouri; Son of Joseph & Jane Couch; Listed in the 1860 Census of Sullivan County (Milan). Married Nancy Frances Foster; Died 1924.

COUCH, William J.; Companies F & A; Rank in: Pvt; Rank out: Pvt; Born 1844 in Sullivan County, Missouri; Son of John & Elizabeth Couch.

CROUSE, Adam; Company A; Rank in: Pvt; Rank out: Pvt; Son of Jacob M. Crouse; Enlisted August 17, 1861 at Sullivan County, Missouri; Mustered into service September 22, 1861; **KIA at the Battle of Shiloh**, Tennessee, April 6, 1862.

CROUSE, John Shannon; Company A; Rank in: Pvt; Rank out: Pvt; Enlisted August 17, 1861 at Sullivan County, Missouri; Mustered in October 8, 1861; Mustered out 18 July 1865 at Louisville, Kentucky; **POW at Battle of Shiloh**; Spent 13 months in Libby Prison, Richmond, Virginia; Born January 1, 1844 in Chippewa Township, Wayne Co., Ohio; Son of Jacob M.

Crouse; Lived in Milan, Sullivan County, Missouri; Married first to Huldah Spake, who died; Married 2nd to Margaret Deeds; Married 3rd to Martha Crouse; Died 7 November 1917 in Polk, Sullivan County, Missouri; Buried at Lovell Cemetery, Polk Township, Sullivan County, Missouri.

DEEDS, Jacob; Company A; Rank in: Pvt; Rank out: Pvt; Born October 10, 1822 in Fairfield County, Ohio; Listed in 1850 and 1860 Census of Sullivan County, Missouri; Lived in Judson, Sullivan County, Missouri; Applied for a disability pension in 1888; Died March 27, 1901; Isabel Deeds applied for a pension as his widow in 1901; Both applications filed in Missouri.

*****DUNLAP, James T. – on memorial stone at Sullivan County Courthouse

Company A; Rank in: Capt; Rank out: Capt; **POW at Battle of Shiloh**; **held at Camp Oglethorpe, Georgia**; Resigned June 27, 1863; Later joined the 44th Missouri Infantry, Company E at 1st Lt.; **Wounded in Battle of Franklin**, Tennessee; Died December 11, 1864; Rosanna Dunlap applied for a pension as his widow in 1865.

James T. Dunlap, born December, 8, 1816 married Mary H. Brown. He was a farmer and they had five children. Mary died and he married Rosanna McCauley. They had six children. He was a soldier in the Mexican war from Sangamon County, Illinois. He moved to Missouri. James Dunlap and his wife "Rosina" are listed in the 1860 Census of Sullivan County, Missouri with their seven children. He is listed as a 44 year old farmer, born in Tennessee; In August, 1861, he was elected Captain of Company A of the 23rd Missouri Volunteers and was **captured at the Battle of Shiloh** on April 6, 1862. He was exchanged after seven months imprisonment, returned home, and later resigned on June 27, 1863. He then served one term in the Missouri Legislature. Later he joined the 44th Missouri Infantry, Company E, and **died from wounds received at the Battle of Franklin**, Tennessee on December 11, 1864, while acting as Captain of his Company.

EASTWOOD, Decalf C.; Company A; Rank in: Pvt; Rank out: Pvt; Born 1838 in Illinois; Married Rachel; Listed in the 1870 Census of Sullivan County, Missouri; Lived in Wintersville.

EATON, Jacob T.; Company A; Rank in: Pvt; Rank out: Pvt; **Wounded in thigh at Battle of Shiloh**; Born February 10, 1834; Son of Elisha & Mary Eaton; Listed in the 1860 Census of Sullivan County, Missouri. Lived in Wintersville. Married Martha Ralls in Sullivan County, Missouri; Applied for a disability pension in 1868 in Missouri; Died in Arkansas; Martha Eaton applied for a pension as his widow with a minor child in 1878 in Missouri.

EATON, James T.; Company A; Rank in: Pvt; Rank out: Pvt; Born March 20, 1840 in Sullivan County, Missouri; Son of Elisha & Mary Eaton; Listed in the 1860 census of Sullivan County, Missouri; Married Ruth Ann Todd on November 11, 1860 in Sullivan County, Missouri; Died February 2, 1911 in Sullivan County, Missouri.

ELLISON, John; Company A; Rank in: Cpl; Rank out: Sgt; Enlisted August 17, 1861; Discharged September 23, 1864; In Battles of Shiloh, Peach Tree Creek, Siege of Atlanta, Jonesboro; Born 1833 in West Virginia; Married Frances Ellison in Sullivan County, Missouri on May 8, 1859; Listed in the 1870 Census of Jackson Township, Sullivan County, Missouri, as a farmer.

HEFLIN, William H.; Company A; Rank in: Pvt; Rank out: Pvt; Born 1840 in Virginia; Married Catharine; Listed in the 1860 Census of Sullivan County, Missouri, as a farmer; Applied for a disability pension in Missouri.

HILL, Benjamin F.; Company A; Rank in: Pvt; Rank out: Pvt; Born 1839 in Missouri; Son of Armstead & Nancy Hill; Listed in the 1860 Census of Sullivan County, Missouri, as a farm hand.

HILL, Leonidas; Company A; Rank in: Pvt; Rank out: Pvt; Born 1842 in Missouri; Son of Armstead & Nancy Hill; Listed in 1860 census in Sullivan County, Missouri.

HUNSAKER, Levi; Companies A & G; Enlisted August 17, 1861; Rank in: Pvt; Mustered September 22, 1861; Transferred to Company G on November 1, 1861; Rank out: Cpl (January 1, 1862); **POW at Battle of Shiloh; paroled May 24, 1862 at Macon, Georgia**; Discharged December 30, 1864; Born 1820; Son of Matthew & Elizabeth Hunsaker; Listed in the 1860 Census of Sullivan County, Missouri; Lived in Unionville, Putnam County, Missouri after the war; Moved to Kincaid, Kansas in 1890; Struck by a train on November 29, 1899 and killed; Buried in Kincaid Cemetery, Kincaid, Kansas; Applied for a disability pension; Prudence Hunsaker applied for a pension as his widow; Both were filed in Kansas.

JOHNSON, Doctor Franklin; Company A; Rank in: Pvt; Rank out: Pvt; **POW at Battle of Shiloh**; Held as prisoner at Montgomery, Alabama; Paroled October 19, 1862 and returned to unit on December 26, 1862; Born about 1836 in Boone County, Missouri; Son of Phillip & Sarah Johnson; Married Esther Mullins; Resided in Milan, Sullivan County, Missouri; Died 1890 in Reger, Sullivan County, Missouri.

JOHNSON, Major; Company A; Rank in: Pvt; Rank out: Pvt; **POW at Battle of Shiloh**; Born January 25, 1844 in Boone County, Missouri; Son of Phillip & Sarah Johnson; Listed in the 1870 Census of Sullivan County, Missouri; Married Mary Russell on August 13, 1865 in Sullivan County, Missouri; Died October 20, 1913 in Linn County, Oregon; Buried at Lebanon Masonic Cemetery, Linn Co., Oregon.

JOHNSON, Richard; Company A; Rank in: Pvt; Rank out: Pvt; Born 1844 in Indiana; Listed in the 1870 Census of Sullivan County, Missouri; Lived in Milan.

KELLER, William P; Company A; Rank in: Pvt; Rank out: Pvt; Born 1832 in Missouri; Son of Jacob & Mary Watson; Listed in the 1860 Census of Sullivan County, Missouri as a farm laborer.

LESLIE, Gabriel; Company A; Rank in: Pvt; Rank out: Pvt; Born 1836 in Ohio; Listed in the 1860 Census of Sullivan County, Missouri, as a farmer; Catharine A. Leslie applied for a pension as his widow in 1863 and 1865.

MARTIN, Marion T.; Company A; Rank in: Pvt; Rank out: Pvt; Enlisted on August 17, 1861; **POW at Battle of Shiloh** on April 6, 1862; Prisoner until October 9, 1862; **Discharged December 7, 1862 for disability**; Born July 10, 1840 in Hancock County, Illinois; Moved with parents to Jamesport, Daviess County, Missouri; Resided in Sullivan County, Missouri for most of his youth; Married Hannah Stout on January 19, 1860; Became a medical doctor; Practiced medicine in Sullivan County, Missouri then to Clark County, Iowa; Died December 29, 1925; Buried at Woodburn, Clark County, Iowa.

*****MAY, Fountain - on memorial stone at Sullivan County Courthouse

Company A; Rank in: Pvt; Rank out: Pvt; **POW in Battle of Shiloh; Died while prisoner at Camp Oglethorpe, Macon, Georgia**; Born in Virginia in 1825; Son of Jacob and Elizabeth May; Moved to Sullivan County about 1858; Listed in the 1860 Census of Sullivan County, Missouri; Virginia May applied for a pension as the widow of Fountain May in 1862.

McCABE, Patrick; Company A; Rank in: Pvt; Born 1846 in Ireland; Son of Michael and Catherine McCabe; Listed in the 1860 census of Sullivan County, Missouri.

*****McCULLOUGH, John - on memorial stone at Sullivan County Courthouse

Rank in: Major; Rank out: Major; **POW in Battle of Shiloh**; Born June 22, 1809 in Pennsylvania; Married Elizabeth Bell on July 17, 1831 in Pennsylvania; Listed in the 1860 Census of Sullivan County, Missouri; Resided in Louisiana, Booneville, Missouri and Sullivan County, Missouri; Died October 7, 1863 at Rolla, Missouri; Buried in Sullivan County, Missouri.

McNABB, Tennessee L.; Company A; Rank in: 1st Sgt; Rank out: Capt; Mustered out September 22, 1864; Born 1832 in Illinois; Married Mary; Listed in the 1860 Census of Sullivan County, Missouri.

MONTGOMERY, Rufus; Company A; Rank in: Pvt; Rank out: Pvt; Listed in the 1860 Census of Sullivan County Missouri; Born 1835 in Ohio; Son of Richard Montgomery; Married Olive, had six children; Listed in the 1860 Census of Sullivan County, Missouri; In the 1880 Census he is listed as a teamster; Applied for a disability pension in 1889; Olive Montgomery applied for a pension as his widow in 1892; Both were filed in Missouri.

MULLINS, David Walter; Company A; Rank in: Pvt; Rank out: Pvt; Mustered out July 18, 1865 at Louisville, Kentucky County, Missouri; Born December 11, 1845; Son of David & Nancy Mullins; Married Priscilla Stone on May 10, 1864 in Sullivan; Killed by gunshot wound to the face while serving as Associate Constable; Died March 5, 1884; Buried at Oakwood Cemetery, Milan, Sullivan Co, Missouri.

MURPHY, James; Company A; Rank in: Pvt; Rank out: Pvt; Born in 1814 in Kentucky; Married Sophia; Listed in the 1870 Census of Sullivan County, Missouri; Lived in Milan.

PRICE, David E.; Company A; Rank in: Pvt; Rank out: Pvt; Born 1831 in Tennessee; Married Liddy; Listed in the 1870 Census of Sullivan County, Missouri; Lived in Milan.

PRIVITT, Willis B.; Company A; Rank in: Sgt; Rank out: Sgt; Born 1819 in North Carolina; Listed in the 1870 Census of Sullivan County, Missouri, as a farm laborer; Married Sarah;

REEVES, John William; Company A; Rank in: Pvt; Rank out: Pvt; Born June 18, 1842 in Brown County, Illinois; Son of Elijah and Margaret Reeves; Married Lydia Dorman on August 3, 1861 in Sullivan County, Missouri; Died March 10, 1917; Buried at Union Cemetery, Union County, Oregon.

REEVES, Thomas Albert; Company A; Rank in: Pvt; Rank out: Pvt; Born August 8, 1844 in Brown County, Illinois; Son of Elijah and Margaret Reeves; Listed in the 1860 Census of Sullivan County, Missouri; Married Frances Baldridge on April 29, 1867 in Sullivan County, Missouri; Lived in Judson, Sullivan County, Missouri; Died August 4, 1905 in Sullivan County, Missouri; Buried at Bairstown Cemetery, Putnam County, Missouri.

ROBBINS, David D.; Company A; **Wounded at Battle of Shiloh**; Born 1840 in Missouri; Married Mary Jane Nowels; Listed in the 1870 Census of Sullivan County, Missouri.

SANDERS, James T.; Company A; Rank in: Sgt; Rank out: Sgt; Born 1833 in Shelby County, Indiana; Son of Henry and Nancy Sanders; Married Martha ("Patsy") Pile on May 1, 1856 in Shelby County, Indiana; Listed in the 1860 Census of Sullivan County, Missouri; **KIA at Battle of Shiloh**; Patsy Sanders applied for a pension as his widow and an application was made on behalf of a minor child in 1864.

SANDERS, William S.; Company A; Rank in: Pvt; Rank out: Pvt; Born January 26, 1828 in Shelby County, Indiana; Son of Henry & Nancy Sanders; Married Rebecca Pile in 1852 in Shelby County, Indiana; Listed in the 1860 Census of Sullivan County, Missouri; Resided in Mercer, Grundy and Sullivan Counties in Missouri; **Died April 26, 1862** in St Louis, Missouri while in still in Army.

*****SEAMAN, William O. - on memorial stone at Sullivan County Courthouse

Company A; Rank in: 2nd Lt; Rank out: 1st Lt; **Killed in Action near Atlanta, Georgia on July 31, 1864**; Born in Indiana in 1833; Listed in the 1860 Census of Sullivan County, Missouri; Susan J. Seaman applied for a pension as his widow in 1864.

SMILEY, Riley M.; Company A; Rank in: Pvt; Rank out: Pvt; Drummer; Born November 27, 1843 in Indiana; Son of Joseph and Parthena Smiley; Listed in the 1860 Census of Sullivan County, Missouri as a farmhand; Married Catherine Muck on November 27, 1864 in Sullivan

County, Missouri; Lived in Wintersville, Sullivan County, Missouri; Applied for a disability pension in Kansas in 1887.

SNAPP, John; Company A; Rank in: Pvt; Rank out: Pvt; Born 1839 in Illinois; Listed in the household of J. H. & Nancy Snapp in the 1860 Census of Medicine Township, Mercer County, Missouri; Married Martha Brantley; Died July 18, 1915 in Harris, Sullivan County, Missouri; Buried at Wintersville Cemetery, Sullivan County, Missouri.

SPENCER, Elijah A.; Company A; Rank in: Pvt; Rank out: Pvt; Born April 20, 1837 in Lee County, Virginia; Son of John & Henrietta Spencer; Married Nancy E. Jones; Listed in the 1860 Census of Sullivan County, Missouri; Died March 13, 1919.

TODD, John K.; Company A; Rank in: Cpl; Rank out: Sgt; Born January 12, 1836; Son of Lewis G. & Elizabeth Todd; Died November 9, 1917; Buried at Union Grove Cemetery, Sullivan County, Missouri.

TODD, Samuel A.; Companies A & G; Rank in: Pvt; Rank out: Pvt; Musician; Born July 16, 1841 in Shelby County, Indiana; Son of Lewis and Elizabeth Todd; Married Harriett Stewart in 1859 in Sullivan County, Missouri; Listed in the 1860 Census of Sullivan County, Missouri; Lived in Humphreys; Died September 16, 1931 in Sullivan County, Missouri.

TUNNELL, Jacob Charles; Company A; Rank in: Pvt; Rank out: Pvt; Born December 13, 1821 in Hawkins Co., Tennessee; Son of John & Elizabeth Tunnell; Married Susannah; Listed in the 1860 Census of Sullivan County, Missouri; **Died August 4, 1862;** Buried at Andersonville National Cemetery, Georgia.

TUNNELL, Josiah R.; Company A; Rank in: Pvt; Rank out: Cpl; Born March 1, 1843 in Hawkins County, Tennessee; Son of John & Elizabeth Tunnell; Listed in the 1860 Census of Sullivan County, Missouri; **Died August 11, 1864 in Nashville, Tennessee;** Buried at Nashville National Cemetery, Nashville, Tennessee.

WAGGONER, John S.; Company A; Rank in: Pvt; Rank out: Pvt; Born 1827 in North Carolina; Married Mary; Listed in the 1860 Census of Sullivan County, Missouri, as a farmer; Mary Waggoner applied for a pension as his widow in 1878.

WEBB, Ephraim L.; Company A; Rank in: 1st Lt; Rank out: 1st Lt; Resigned February 2, 1863 and transferred to the 44th Missouri Infantry; Born 1820 in Indiana; Listed in the 1860 Census of Wintersville Township, Sullivan County, Missouri, as a blacksmith; Elizabeth J. Todd applied for a pension as his widow in Missouri.

MEN FROM THE 23rd MISSOURI VOLUNTEER INFANTRY

KNOWN TO HAVE BEEN HELD AT

CAMP OGLETHORPE, MACON, GEORGIA

Although most of the prisoners captured at the Battle of Shiloh were taken to Camp Oglethorpe, Macon, Georgia, these men are confirmed to have been there.

BROWN, George W.; Company E; Rank in: 2Lt; Rank out: 2Lt; **POW at Battle of Shiloh; Escaped from POW camp at Macon, GA;** Resigned Jul 8, 1863;

CAMP, Judson N.; Company F; Rank in: 1Lt; Rank out: Lt; **POW at Battle of Shiloh; Escaped from POW Camp at Macon, GA;** Killed in Action near Atlanta, GA on Aug 4, 1864.

CRUMP, Richard W.; Company F; Rank in: Pvt; Rank out: Pvt; **POW in Battle of Shiloh; Died while prisoner at Camp Oglethorpe, Macon, GA;** Richard W. Crump is listed in the 1860 Census of Sullivan County, Missouri in the household of his father, Richard Crump; He is listed as a 22 year old laborer, born in Illinois.

DILLON, Joseph A. Ketcham; Company B; Rank in: Cpl; Rank out: Cpl; Enlisted Aug 26, 1861; **Captured at Battle of Shiloh; Died of chronic diarrhea at Camp Oglethorpe (POW Camp), Macon GA Aug 22, 1862;** Born Jan 25, 1837; Son of William & Eleanor Dillon; Married Sarah Priest on May 15, 1856 in Grundy County, Missouri.

DUNLAP, James T.; Company A; Rank in: Capt; Rank out: Capt; **POW at Battle of Shiloh; held at Camp Oglethorpe, Georgia;** Resigned June 27, 1863; Later joined the 44th Missouri Infantry, Company E at 1st Lt.; Wounded in Battle of Franklin, Tennessee; Died Dec 11, 1864; Rosanna Dunlap applied for a pension as his widow in 1865.

HUNSAKER, Levi; Companies A & G; Enlisted August 17, 1861; Rank in: Pvt; Mustered September 22, 1861; Transferred to Company G on November 1, 1861; Rank out: Cpl (January 1, 1862); **POW at Battle of Shiloh; paroled May 24, 1862 at Macon, Georgia;** Discharged December 30, 1864; Born 1836 in Illinois; Son of Matthew & Elizabeth Hunsaker; Resided in Sullivan County, Missouri; Lived in Unionville, Putnam County, Missouri after the war; Moved to Kincaid, Kansas in 1890; Struck by a train on November 29, 1899 and killed; Buried at Kincaid Cemetery, Kincaid, Kansas; Applied for a disability pension; Prudence Hunsaker applied for a pension as his widow; both were filed in Kansas.

HURST, Samuel Albert; Company A; Rank in: Pvt; Rank out: Pvt; **Died while a prisoner at Macon, Georgia;** Son of William & Elizabeth Hurst.

KETCHAM, Joseph A.; Company B; Rank in: Cpl; Rank out: Cpl; **POW at Battle of Shiloh; Died at Camp Oglethorpe, Macon Georgia on August 22, 1862.**

MAY, Fountain; Company A; Rank in: Pvt; Rank out: Pvt; **POW in Battle of Shiloh; Died while prisoner at Camp Oglethorpe, Macon, Georgia**; Born in Virginia in 1825; son of Jacob and Elizabeth May; moved to Sullivan County about 1858; Fountain May is listed in the 1860 Census of Sullivan County, Missouri as born in Virginia, 33 years old; Virginia May applied for a pension as the widow of Fountain May in 1862.

McCALLISTER, Thomas; Company A; Rank in: Cpl; Rank out: 1st Sgt; Enlisted July 6, 1861; **POW in Battle of Shiloh; Paroled from Macon, Georgia;** Re-joined his regiment in 1863; Marched with Sherman to the sea; Wounded July 27 1864; Discharged September 1864.

SWOPES, Ames John (Some records list him as John Ames Swope); Company C; Rank in: Pvt; Rank out: Pvt; POW in Battle of Shiloh; **Died while prisoner at Camp Oglethorpe, Macon, GA on August 21, 1862 of wounds received at Battle of Shiloh; B**orn in Missouri; Son of James & Ruth Swopes; Listed in the 1860 Census of Medicine Township, Mercer County, Missouri as a farm laborer.

MEN OF THE 23RD MISSOURI INFANTRY
who were POWs at the Battle of Shiloh
They were possibly held at Camp Oglethorpe

ANDERSON, Garret N.; Company F; Rank in: Pvt; Rank out: Pvt; **POW at Battle of Shiloh.**

ANDERSON, John G.; Company F; Rank in: Pvt ; Rank out: Pvt; **POW at Battle of Shiloh.**

AUBERRY, Thomas; Companies F& A; Rank in: Pvt; Rank out: Pvt; **POW at Battle of Shiloh**.

BAKER, William; Company K; Rank in: Sgt; Rank out: Sgt; **POW at Battle of Shiloh**.

BALDWIN, James R.; Company C; Rank in: Pvt; Rank out: Pvt; **POW at Battle of Shiloh;** Escaped and was recaptured.

BENDER, John W.; Company E; Rank in: Pvt; Rank out: Pvt; **POW,** Paroled December 19, 1862; Died January 7, 1863 of smallpox at Baltimore, Maryland.

BISHOP, Isaac; Company G; Rank in: Cpl; Rank out: Cpl; **POW at Battle of Shiloh;** Medical discharge on October 23, 1862; Died August 25, 1864 at Carrolton, Missouri.

BROCK, Bennett H.; Company K; Rank in: Pvt; Rank out: Pvt; Wounded and **POW at Battle of Shiloh;** Paroled May 22, 1862; Born about 1827; Son of Joel & Martha Brock; Married Rebecca Standley in Carroll County, Missouri; Died August 25, 1864; Rebecca Brock applied for pension as widow in 1872.

BROWN, Charles Hadley; Company H; Rank in: Sgt; Rank out: Sgt; **POW at Battle of Shiloh;** Born November 5, 1838 in Indiana; Son of Jacob & Sarah Brown; Married Julia Long on December 22, 1853 in Grundy County, Missouri; Resided in Harrison and Daviess Counties in Missouri; Died June 23, 1913; Buried Bainbridge Cemetery, Harlan County, Nebraska.

BROWN, George W.; Company E; Rank in: 2Lt; Rank out: 2Lt; **POW at Battle of Shiloh; Escaped from POW camp at Macon, Georgia;** Resigned July 8, 1863.

BURT, Grandison W.; Company F; Rank in: Pvt; Rank out: Cpl; **POW at Battle of Shiloh.**

CAMP, Judson N.; Company F; Rank in: 1Lt; Rank out: Lt; **POW at Battle of Shiloh; Escaped from POW Camp at Macon, Georgia;** Killed in Action near Atlanta, Georgia on August 4, 1864.

COTTER, Andrew J.; Company F; Rank in: Pvt; Rank out: Pvt; **POW at Battle of Shiloh;** Born March 31, 1842; Son of Stephen & Elizabeth Cotter; Listed in 1860 Census of Linn County in the household of his father; Married Nancy Ellen Pipes; Resided in Linn County, Missouri; Died October 31, 1920; Burial Jenkins Cemetery, Linn Co., Missouri.

COTTER, Sidney; Company F; Rank in: Pvt; Rank out: Pvt; **POW at Battle of Shiloh.**

COTTER, William Ellison; Company F; Rank in: Pvt; Rank out: Cpl; **POW at Battle of Shiloh;** Born in Tennessee; William, wife Mary and children are listed in the 1860 Census of Linn county, Missouri; William Ellison Cotter applied for disability pension in 1880; Mary P. Cotter applied for a pension as his widow in 1893.

COTTER, William M., Jr.; Company F; Rank in: Pvt; Rank out: Pvt; **POW at Battle of Shiloh;** Born in Tennessee; Lived in Linn County, Missouri.

COUCH, Daniel Stewart; Company F; Rank in: Pvt; Rank out: Pvt; **POW at Battle of Shiloh;** Born October 2, 1839 in Sullivan County, Missouri; Son of Joseph & Jane Couch; Daniel S. Couch applied for a disability pension in 1888 in Kansas; Died November 25, 1911 Canadian County, Oklahoma; Mary A. Couch applied for a pension as his widow in 1911 in Oklahoma.

CROUSE, John Shannon; Company A; Rank in: Pvt; Rank out: Pvt; **POW at Battle of Shiloh;** John Crouse applied for a disability pension in 1888; Martha Crouse applied for a pension as his widow in 1907; Both were filed in Missouri.

CRUMP, Daniel Ira; Company F; Rank in: Pvt; Rank out: Pvt; **POW at Battle of Shiloh;** Prisoner held at Andersonville, Georgia (Unconfirmed); Born in 1843 in Illinois; Son of Richard Crump; Listed in the 1860 Census of Sullivan County, Missouri.

CUMMINS, Lewis; Company E; Rank in: Pvt; Rank out: Pvt; **POW at Battle of Shiloh.**

DALE, Reuben; Company D; Rank in: Cpl; Rank out: Cpl; Enlisted in Harrison County, Missouri; Mustered in September 22, 1861; **POW at Battle of Shiloh;** Born 1835; Son of Reuben & Patsy Dale; Died in 1864 in Atlanta, Georgia.

DANIEL, Charles Franklin; Company E; Rank in: Pvt; Rank out: Pvt; **POW at Battle of Shiloh;** Born November 20, 1839; Died July 23, 1871; Buried at Daniel Cemetery, Harrison County, Missouri.

DANIEL, John Gideon; Company E; Rank in: Pvt; Rank out: Pvt; **POW at Battle of Shiloh;** Born February 11, 1840 in Morgan County, Illinois; Son of Thomas & Chloe (Shofner) Daniel; Died October 15, 1911; Buried at White Oak Cemetery, Harrison County, Missouri.

DANIEL, Thomas Jackson; Company E; Rank in: Pvt; Rank out: Pvt; **POW at Battle of Shiloh;** Born in Illinois on December 26, 1837; Son of William & Polly Daniel; Died December 21, 1899.

DANIEL, William Alfred; Company E; Rank in: Pvt; Rank out: Pvt; Enlisted August 3, 1861; **POW at Battle of Shiloh;** Born in Illinois in 1836; Son of William & Polly Daniel; Married Mary Querry on February 16, 1871; Died December 21, 1899.

DAVIS, George; Company F; Rank in: Pvt; Rank out: Pvt; **POW at Battle of Shiloh.**

DAVIS, James T; Company B; Rank in: Pvt; Rank out: Pvt; Drummer; **POW at Battle of Shiloh;** Discharged due to disability on September 1, 1862; Born February 11, 1842 in Allen County, Ohio; Son of John Davis (1st Sgt); Died November 17, 1917; Buried at Richardson Cemetery; Grundy County, Missouri.

DeBOLT, Renzin; Companies A & B; Rank in: Lt; Rank out: Capt; **POW at Battle of Shiloh;** Elected Capt of Company B after Battle of Shiloh; Resigned March 1863; Born January 20, 1828; Died October 29, 1891; Burial I.O.O.F. Cemetery, Grundy County, Missouri.

DODGE, Vincent; Company F; Rank in: Pvt; Rank out: Pvt; **POW at Battle of Shiloh;** Son of Lewis & Eliza Dodge; Married Ara; Applied for a disability pension; Ara Dodge applied for a widow's pension and for her minor child, John.

DORSEY, John C.; Company K; Rank in Pvt; Rank out: Pvt; **POW at Battle of Shiloh; Died while POW;** America Dorsey applied for widow's pension and for her minor child, R. P.

DRINKARD, George W.; Company H; Rank in: Fifer; Rank out: Pvt; **POW at Battle of Shiloh;** Later held at Andersonville Prison; Paroled April 16, 1865; Applied for disability pension on October 20, 1888 in Kansas; Listed in 1860 Census in Grundy County, Missouri.

EVERETT, Elisha J.; Company I; Rank in: Pvt; Rank out: Pvt; **POW at Battle of Shiloh;** Possibly held prisoner at Andersonville, Georgia; Born March 24, 1845 in Mercer County, Missouri; Died August 18, 1910; Buried at McKee Cemetery, Hallowell, Kansas.

GRAY, R.; Company E; Rank in: Pvt; Rank out: Pvt; **POW at Battle of Shiloh.**

HARPER, John J.; Company E; Rank in: Pvt; Rank out: 2nd Lt; **POW at Battle of Shiloh;** Died September 22, 1864; Comfort Harper applied for a widow's pension in 1864 in Missouri.

HEDRIX, Samuel Henry; Companies C & K; Rank in: Lt; Rank out: 2nd Lt; **POW at Battle of Shiloh;** Held prisoner at Andersonville, Georgia; Re-enlisted into Company K in 1864; Born May 16, 1845 in Clay County, Kentucky; Son of William & Temperance Hedrix; Married Polly Baker, August 10, 1865 in Grundy County, Missouri; Resided near Goshen, Mercer County, Missouri; Died August 14, 1933; Buried at Allerton Cemetery, Wayne County, Iowa.

HOOKER, John Becket; Companies F & C; Rank in: Pvt; Rank out: Pvt; **POW at Battle of Shiloh;** Born May 7, 1837 in Linn County, Missouri; Son of Jeremiah & Mary Hooker; Married Margaret Hatcher; Died June 20, 1917 in Mercer County, Missouri.

HOOVER, John Henry; Company H; Rank in Pvt; Rank out: Pvt; **POW at Battle of Shiloh;** Enlisted at age 15; Born June 5, 1847 in Daviess County, Missouri; Son of James and Elizabeth Hoover; Married Nancy Hysell on April 5, 1871 in Santa Clara County, California; Died January 30, 1916; Buried at Santa Clara, California.

HOSKINS, Jasper; Company F; Rank in: Pvt; Rank out: Pvt; **POW at Battle of Shiloh;** Born 1834 in Missouri; Son of Thomas & Mary Hoskins; Married Mary; Listed in 1860 census of Sullivan County, Missouri, a farmer; Died 1862, shortly after Battle of Shiloh.

HOWREY, Charles S.; Company E; Rank in: Pvt; Rank out: Pvt; **POW at Battle of Shiloh;** Applied for disability pension; Rebecca A. Howrey applied for widow's pension.

HUNSAKER, Levi; Companies A & G; Enlisted August 17, 1861; Rank in: Pvt; Mustered September 22, 1861; Transferred to Company G on November 1, 1861; Rank out: Cpl (January 1, 1862); **POW at Battle of Shiloh**; paroled May 24, 1862 at Macon, Georgia; Discharged December 30, 1864; Born 1820; Son of Matthew & Elizabeth Hunsaker; Listed in the 1860 Census of Sullivan County, Missouri; Lived in Unionville, Putnam County, Missouri after the war; Moved to Kincaid, Kansas in 1890; Struck by a train on November 29, 1899 and killed; Buried at Kincaid Cemetery, Kincaid, Kansas; Applied for a disability pension; Prudence Hunsaker applied for a pension as his widow; Both were filed in Kansas.

JOHNSON, Doctor Franklin; Company A; Rank in: Pvt; Rank out: Pvt; **POW at Battle of Shiloh**; Held as prisoner at Montgomery, Alabama; Paroled October 19, 1862 and returned to unit on December 26, 1862; Born about 1836 in Boone County, Missouri; Son of Phillip & Sarah Johnson; Married Esther Mullins; Resided in Milan, Sullivan County, Missouri; Died 1890 in Reger, Sullivan County, Missouri.

JOHNSON, Major; Company A; Rank in: Pvt; Rank out: Pvt; **POW at Battle of Shiloh**; Born January 25, 1844 in Boone County, Missouri; Son of Phillip & Sarah Johnson; Listed in the 1870 Census of Sullivan County, Missouri; Married Mary Russell on August 13, 1865 in Sullivan County, Missouri; Died October 20, 1913 in Linn County, Oregon; Buried at Lebanon Masonic Cemetery, Linn Co., Oregon.

LANE; Lawson R.; Company K; Rank in: Sgt; Rank out: 2nd Lt; **POW at Battle of Shiloh;** Mustered out January 17, 1865; Born 1843 in Indiana; Son of Elijah & Susanna Lane; Listed in the 1860 Census of Carroll County, Missouri.

LEAR, William; Company E; Rank in: Pvt; Rank out: Pvt; **POW at Battle of Shiloh;** Born 1844 in Indiana; Son of Joseph & Martha Lear; Lived in Butler Township, Harrison County, Missouri.

MARSH, Henry Judson; Company D; Rank in: Pvt; Rank out: Pvt; **POW at Battle of Shiloh;** Born 1834 in Ohio; Listed in the 1860 Census of Lindley Township, Mercer County, Missouri, as a farm laborer; Married Georgia Lovett; Died October 20, 1914; Buried at Dobson Cemetery, Tama County, Iowa.

MARTIN, John A.; Company E; Rank in: Sgt; Rank out: 1st Lt; **POW at Battle of Shiloh;** Mustered out September 22, 1864.

MARTIN, Marion T.; Company A; Rank in: Pvt; Rank out: Pvt; Enlisted on August 17, 1861; **POW at Battle of Shiloh**; Prisoner until October 9, 1862; Discharged December 7, 1862 for disability; Born July 10, 1840 in Hancock County, Illinois; Moved with parents to Jamesport, Daviess County, Missouri; Resided in Sullivan County, Missouri for most of his youth; Married Hannah Stout on January 19, 1860; Became a medical doctor; Practiced medicine in Sullivan County, Missouri then to Clark County, Iowa; Died December 29, 1925; Buried at Woodburn, Clark County, Iowa.

MAXEY, Bazel M.; Company F; Rank in: Pvt; Rank out Pvt; **POW at Battle of Shiloh.**

McCALLISTER, Thomas W.; Company A; Rank in: Cpl; Rank out: 1st Sgt; Ord Sgt; **POW at Battle of Shiloh;** Thomas McCallister applied for a disability pension; Margaret McCallister applied for a pension as his widow; Both were filed in Missouri.

McCULLOUGH, John; Company A; Rank in: Major; Rank out: Major; **POW at Battle of Shiloh**; Born June 22, 1809 in Pennsylvania; Married Elizabeth Bell on July 17, 1831 in Pennsylvania; Listed in the 1860 Census of Sullivan County, Missouri; Resided in Louisiana, Booneville, Missouri and Sullivan County, Missouri; Died October 7, 1863 at Rolla, Missouri; Buried in Sullivan County, Missouri.

McKAY, Charles J.; Company F; Rank in: Pvt; Rank out: Cpl; **POW at Battle of Shiloh.**

MILLER, Jacob E.; Company E; Rank in: Pvt; Rank out: Pvt; **POW at Battle of Shiloh;** Applied for a pension in 1890; An application was made on behalf of his minor daughter in 1889.

MILLSPAW, Mathew; Company E; Rank in: Pvt; Rank out: Pvt; **POW at Battle of Shiloh;** Born in Michigan; Married Delilah Miller; Listed in the 1860 Census of Marshall County, Kansas Territory, a day laborer.

MODRELL, James S.; Company I; Rank in: Cpl; Rank out: Cpl; **POW at Battle of Shiloh;** Mustered out July 19, 1865; Born January 12, 1829 in Owen County, Indiana; Son of John & Margaret Modrell; Married Catherine Friend; Died April 21, 1870; Listed in the 1860 Census of Chariton County, Missouri.

MOORE, Samuel J.; Company D; Rank in: Sgt; Rank out: Sgt; **POW at Battle of Shiloh.**

MOORE, William H.; Company F; Rank in: Pvt; Rank out: Pvt; **POW at Battle of Shiloh;** Born 1842 in Tennessee; Son of Amos & Ruth Moore; Died July 4, 1879 in Linn County, Missouri.

MORGAN, Allen M. C. D.; Company D; Rank in: Pvt; Rank out: Pvt ; **POW at Battle of Shiloh;** Buried at Jones Chapel Cemetery, Harrison County, Missouri.

MORRIS, Hiram; Company B; Rank in: Pvt; Rank out: Pvt; **POW at Battle of Shiloh**; Born 1847; Died 1872; Buried at Groff Cemetery, Grundy County, Missouri.

MULLEN, John W.; Company H; Rank in: Pvt; Rank out: Pvt; **POW at Battle of Shiloh.**

MURPHY, Thomas B.; Company E; Rank in: Pvt; Rank out: Pvt; **POW at Battle of Shiloh.**

MURRY, Jeremiah; Company K; Rank in: Pvt; Rank out: Pvt; **POW at Battle of Shiloh.**

NOAH, J.; Company E; Rank in: Pvt; Rank out: Pvt; POW **at Battle of Shiloh**; Born August 10, 1844; Son of John & Sarah Noah; Married Margaret Murphy; Resided in Kirksville, Adair County, Missouri; Died July 21, 1913; Buried at Old City Cemetery, Garnet, Kansas.

OGLE, William; Company F; Rank in: Pvt; Rank out: Pvt; **POW at Battle of Shiloh**; Born in 1824 in Tennessee; Married Lucinda; Listed in the 1860 Census of Putnam County, Missouri, a carpenter.

PARKERSON, J.; Company E; Rank in: Pvt; Rank out: Pvt; **POW at Battle of Shiloh.**

PARKEY, William H.; Company F; Rank in: Pvt; Rank out: Pvt; **POW in Battle of Shiloh**; Died May 20, 1864 in POW camp at Tuscaloosa, Alabama.

PEERY, James W.; Company F; Rank in: Pvt; Rank out: Pvt; **POW at Battle of Shiloh.**

PHILBERT, Wharton B.; Company F; Rank in: Pvt; Rank out: Pvt; **POW at Battle of Shiloh**; Born 1843 in Indiana; Son of Luke & Hannah Philbert; From Linn Co., Missouri; Died February 23, 1916 in Monterey Co., California.

PHILLIPS, John; Company F; Rank in: Pvt; Rank out: Pvt; **POW at Battle of Shiloh.**

PHILLIPS, Lewis; Company F; Rank in: Pvt; Rank out: Pvt; **POW at Battle of Shiloh.**

REYNOLDS, William F.; Company F; Rank in: Sgt; Rank out: 2Lt; **POW at Battle of Shiloh**; Mustered out December 30, 1864; Applied for a disability pension; Mary A. Reynolds applied for a widow's pension; Both were filed in Oregon.

RICE, Francis M.; Company E; Rank in: Pvt; Rank out: Pvt; **POW at Battle of Shiloh**; Born Jun 15, 1841 in Indiana; Son of William P. & Anna Rice; Died September 8, 1884; Buried near Pattonsburg, Daviess County, Missouri.

ROSS, Abraham; Company F; Rank in: Pvt; Rank out: Pvt; **POW at Battle of Shiloh.**

SIMMS, William R.; Company E; Rank in: Lt; Rank out: Capt; **POW at Battle of Shiloh;** Born 1836 in Ohio; Married Elizabeth; Listed in the 1860 Census of Butler Township, Harrison County, Missouri, a school teacher; John Arnold applied for a pension as the guardian of a minor child of William R. Simms in 1891 in Missouri.

SISSON, Hiram A.; Company F; Rank in: Cpl; Rank out: Pvt; Musician; **POW at Battle of Shiloh;** Hiram Sisson married Laura Gilstrap on May 24, 1882 in Macon County, Missouri; Applied for a disability pension in 1883; Laura Sisson applied for a widow's pension; Both were filed in Missouri.

SMITH, William; Company F; Rank in: Pvt; Rank out: Pvt; **POW at Battle of Shiloh.**

STINSON, Andrew Jackson; Company D; Rank in: Pvt; Rank out: Pvt; **POW at Battle of Shiloh;** Born December 21, 1836 in Hamilton County, Indiana; Son of Reuben & Sarah Stinson; Married Nancy; Died November 21, 1914 in Lyon County, Kansas; Buried at Maplewood Cemetery, Lyon County, Kansas; Listed in the 1860 Census of Marion Township, Harrison County, Missouri as a farmer; Applied for a disability pension; Nancy E. Stinson applied for a widow's pension.

STONE, David C.; Company F; Rank in: Pvt; Rank out: Pvt; **POW at Battle of Shiloh;** Born 1836 in Ohio; Son of John & Susannah Stone; Died 1877; Listed in the 1860 Census of Livingston County, Missouri, a farmer.

TABLER, Christopher Ausbury; Company G; Rank in: Pvt; Rank out: Pvt; **POW at Battle of Shiloh;** Reenlisted as Veteran Reserve in January, 1864; Born February 10, 1813 in Maryland; Son of Christian and Sarah Tabler; Married Mary; Died December 20, 1873; Listed in the 1860 Census of Carroll County, Missouri, a farmer.

THOMPSON, James C.; Company F; Rank in: Pvt; Rank out: Pvt; **POW at Battle of Shiloh.**

VanBIBER, W.; Company F; Rank in: Pvt; Rank out: Pvt; **POW at Battle of Shiloh.**

VanDYKE, Griffin; Company H; Rank in: Pvt; Rank out: Pvt; **POW at the Battle of Shiloh;** Born September 12, 1842 in Tazwell County, Virginia; Son of John VanDike who also served in the 23rd; Farmed in Mercer County, Missouri; Discharged at Atlanta, Georgia on September 22, 1864; Applied for a disability pension in Nebraska; Died October 25, 1920 in Harlan County, Nebraska.

VINCENT, Wesley V.; Company E; Rank in: Pvt; Rank out: Pvt; **POW at Battle of Shiloh.**

WALKER, Abraham F.; Company I; Rank in: Pvt; Rank out: Pvt; **POW at Battle of Shiloh.**

WASHBURN, Joseph H.; Company I; Rank in: Pvt; Rank out: Pvt; **POW at Battle of Shiloh;** Transferred to Company C on January 14, 1865 when regiment was reorganized; Born 1836 in Michigan; Applied for a disability pension in Kansas. Listed in the 1870 Census of Macon County, Missouri.

WATSON, Washington W.; Company E; Rank in: Pvt; Rank out: Pvt; **POW at Battle of Shiloh;** Born August 6, 1840 in Kentucky; Son of Richard & Lucy Watkins; Married to Nancy Jane Burris; Listed in the 1860 Census of Butler Township, Harrison County, Missouri, a farmer; Died December 2, 1873 of complications from war wounds; Buried at Matkins Cemetery, Harrison Co., Missouri.

WELCH, John; Company F; Rank in: Pvt; Rank out: Pvt; **POW at Battle of Shiloh.**

WELKER, Isaac; Company F; Rank in: Pvt; Rank out: Pvt; **POW at Battle of Shiloh.**

WELSH, Anthony; Company G; Rank in: Pvt; Rank out: Pvt; Enlisted January 14, 1862 in Chillicothe, Missouri; **POW at Battle of Shiloh;** Held at Montgomery, Alabama in May, 1862; Paroled at Atkins Landing, Virginia on October 19, 1862; Mustered out January 24, 1865 at Savannah Georgia; Mary A. Welsh applied for a pension as his widow in Texas.

WILLIAMS, Richard; Company A; Rank in: Pvt; Rank out: Pvt; **POW at Battle of Shiloh.**

WRIGHT, Martin VanBuren; Company F; Rank in: Pvt; Rank out: Pvt; **POW at Battle of Shiloh;** Born April 2, 1837 in Indiana; Son of Hiram & Nancy Wright; Married Hannah Petty on Oct 28, 1858 in Princeton, Mercer County, Missouri; Moved to Wayne County, Iowa about 1862, then to Nebraska about 1885; Died February 24, 1914 in Oklahoma. Buried at Black Cemetery, Lincoln County, Oklahoma.

CASUALTIES OF THE 23rd MISSOURI INFANTRY

Killed: officers 2; men 7
Died of Wounds: men 5
Died of Disease: officers 4; men 47
Discharged for Disability: men 20
Deserted: officers 1; men 83
Missing in Action: men 20
Resigned: officers 33
Honorably Discharged: officers 33; men 748

At the Shiloh National Military Park in Shiloh, Tennessee, these markers have been erected by Shiloh National Military Park Commission in honor the 23rd Missouri Infantry

Inscription Reads: U.S. 23d MISSOURI INFANTRY, PRENTISS' (6th) DIVISION, ARMY OF THE TENNESSEE. This regiment reported to General Prentiss for duty at 9 AM April 6, 1862 and was engaged here until 4 PM when it fell back 200 yards.

U. S. 23d MISSOURI INFANTRY, PRENTISS (6th) DIVISION, ARMY OF THE TENNESSEE.

20 officers and 390 men of this regiment were surrounded and captured here at 5.30 PM April 6, 1862

There is also a marker where the Hornet's Nest battle was fought

CHAIN OF COMMAND

Pvt. Fountain S. May (POW)

Corporals: Charles Adams, John Brown, John Ellison, Benjamin Ford, Thomas McAllister, Noah McCool, Abraham Myers, Arenton Ralls, William Stewart, John H. Todd

Sergeants: James Cookman, John W. Moore, Willis Privitt, James Sanders, John Trowsdale

1st Sergeant: Tennessee McNabb

Lieutenant: James Gyles, Ephraim Webb

2nd Lieutenant Wm. O. Seamon (KIA)

Captains: James Dunlap, Lucien Eaton, George Van Beek

Major John McCullough (POW)

Major John McCullough was born June 22, 1809. He married Elizabeth Bell on Jul 17, 1831 in Pittsburg, Alleghany County, Pennsylvania on July 7, 1831. He resided in Louisiana, Booneville, Missouri and Sullivan County, Missouri. John McCullough was enrolled on the 26th day of Aug 1861 at Milan Missouri in the 23rd Regiment of Missouri Volunteers to serve a term of 3 years or during the war. He mustered into service as a Major on the 1st day of Dec 1861 at Chillicothe, Missouri. He was taken prisoner in the Battle of Shiloh. On Muster Roll for his regiment, he is reported as a Major who died of typhoid fever at Rolla, Missouri on the 7th of October, 1863. He is buried in Sullivan County, Missouri.

Lt. Colonel Quin Morton

Lt. Colonel Quin Legrand Morton, Company F & S, 23rd Missouri Infantry. Rank in: Lt. Colonel; Rank out: Lt. Colonel; Mustered out Jan 17, 1865; born November 8, 1823 in Prince Edward County, Virginia; married Elizabeth Ann Logan; lived in Adair and Lafayette Counties, Missouri; died March 12, 1878 in Shelby County, Kentucky.

Col. Jacob Torian Tindall (KIA)

Col. Jacob T. Tindall was born in Kentucky on April 25, 1826, son of James and Barbara Tindall. He served in the Mexican War in 1847. He was married to Emeline Merrill on March 1, 1849 and they had four children. He was elected a member of the House of Representatives of Missouri in February, 1861. He was an attorney in Trenton, Grundy County, Missouri from 1852 and served on the Missouri Constitutional Convention, which decided that the State of Missouri would remain in the Union. Jacob Tindall organized 1000 men from northwest Missouri in answer to President Lincoln's call for men. He was Colonel of the 23rd Missouri Volunteer Infantry, Company F. He was killed in action at the Battle of Shiloh and buried in Trenton, Grundy County, Missouri.

Brig General Benjamin Prentiss (POW)

Gen. Benjamin Prentiss was born in Belleville, Virginia on November 23, 1819. He was a direct descendant of Valentine Prentice, who emigrated from England in 1631. His early childhood was spent in Virginia until his family joined the migration and moved near Hannibal, Missouri. They then moved to Quincy, Illinois where Prentiss made his home until 1879. He then moved to Missouri.

In his early life, Prentiss was a rope-maker and served as an auctioneer. On March 29, 1838, he married Margaret Ann Lodousky; they had seven children before she died in 1860. In 1862, he married Mary Worthington Whitney, who bore him five more children.

He fought in the Mexican-American War. Prentiss ran unsuccessfully for United States Congress in 1860. At the beginning of the American Civil War he defended railroad lines in Missouri until ordered to command a division under Ulysses S. Grant. His division was the first one attacked at Shiloh and suffered greatly during the opening hours of that battle. Prentiss reformed his command and put up a spirited fight in the "Hornet's Nest".

He was captured at the Hornet's Nest along with 2,200 other Union soldiers. He surrendered his sword to Lt. Colonel Francis M. Walker of the 19th Tennessee Infantry. After the battle he was considered a hero, having held off the Confederate States Army long enough to allow General

Grant to organize a counterattack and win the battle. Grant would later play down Prentiss' role in the victory, possibly because of mutual dislike between the two generals. However, Grant said in his memoirs "Prentiss' command was gone as a division, many of its members having been killed, wounded or captured; but it had rendered valiant services before its final dispersal, and had contributed a good share to the defense of Shiloh".

After being released as part of a prisoner exchange, Prentiss was promoted to major general and served on the court-martial board that convicted Fitz John Porter. His dissenting voice in the final vote damaged his political clout. Prentiss was sent to Arkansas and won the Battle of Helena on July 4, 1863. In 1864, he resigned to tend to his family. Historian Ezra J. Warner speculated that Prentiss felt that he was being shelved after having proved his abilities at Shiloh and Helena.

After the Civil War, Prentiss became a lawyer. He was later appointed as postmaster of Bethany, Missouri, by President Benjamin Harrison and was re-appointed by President William McKinley. He was a leader in the Republican Party of Missouri.

He died in Bethany, Missouri in 1901 and is buried there in Miriam Cemetery, Harrison County, Missouri.[22]

"On the pages of history his name will appear as one whose bravery and indomitable courage hung the fate of Shiloh Battlefield, and, perhaps, the fate of a nation; a man who knew what was right, and dared to tell it as he believed it . . . " --From a resolution passed by the Missouri Legislature upon the death of major General Benjamin M. Prentiss.

Prentiss Headquarters marker at the Shiloh National Military Park, Shiloh, Tennessee

---

[22] Wikipedia, Aug, 2011

Major General Ulysses S. Grant

"Ulysses Grant was born in Ohio, the first of six children. He was small, sensitive, quiet, and well-known for his talent with horses. He attended the United States Military Academy at West Point and excelled in mathematics, writing, drawing, and horsemanship. After graduating, he was assigned to an infantry company in Missouri. His company soon moved south to prepare for the conflict brewing with Mexico over the Texas territory. From 1846 to 1848, Grant fought in the Mexican War and was twice cited for bravery.

After the war, Grant moved to various Army postings in Detroit, New York, and the Pacific Northwest. He resigned suddenly from the Army in 1854 and returned to the Midwest to be with his family. Grant then attempted a variety of jobs, including farming and insurance sales, before finding work in his family's leather goods store in Galena, Illinois. Through these difficult times, he relied on his wife, Julia Dent Grant. The two were a devoted couple and adoring parents to their four children.

When the American Civil War began in 1861, experienced officers like Grant were in short supply. The Illinois governor assigned him to make a disciplined fighting unit out of a rebellious Illinois volunteer regiment. Grant drilled the men, instituted badly needed discipline, and soon earned the respect of the volunteers. The Army noted his efforts and promoted him to brigadier general.

Grant garnered attention as he led his troops to fight and win battles in the western theater. He captured Fort Henry and Fort Donelson, forced the surrender of Vicksburg, Mississippi, and defeated a larger Southern force at Chattanooga. He was both praised and criticized for his willingness to fight because it often cost a disproportionate number of casualties. Grant helped end the bloody Civil War when he led Union troops to trap the main Confederate Army west of Richmond, Virginia and forced its surrender in April 1865. At that point, General Grant was the most revered man in the Union.

Lincoln's tragic assassination at the end of the Civil War was followed by the ineffective leadership of President Andrew Johnson. Johnson urged a moderate approach to Reconstruction that would not punish the South or protect the rights of the newly freed slaves. Radical Republicans wanted to protect the civil and political rights of African Americans. In the election of 1868, postwar social and economic policies were the major campaign issues. The Republicans backed Grant, who concluded his acceptance speech with "Let us have peace." The popular general won the election to become the nation's eighteenth President.

Coming into office, President Grant alienated party stalwarts by eschewing party politics. When he appointed his cabinet, he did not turn to Republicans for their advice. Instead, he chose people he thought he could trust and to whom he could delegate responsibility. This strategy led to some good cabinet appointments but also to a number of dubious ones. Grant was also loyal out of all proportion to anyone who had helped him or worked with him. As a result, he was sometimes unwilling to remove ineffective people, and some areas of his administration suffered from incompetence and corruption.

In his first inaugural address, Grant spoke of his desire for the ratification of the Fifteenth Amendment, which sought to grant citizens the right to vote regardless of race or previous servitude. He lobbied hard to get the amendment passed, angering many Southern whites in the process. He also, on occasion, sent in the military to protect African Americans from newly formed terrorist groups, such as the Ku Klux Klan, which tried to prevent blacks from participating in society. Grant incurred the wrath of citizens who blamed him for the economic woes that plagued the nation in the aftermath of the war. In 1872, however, Grant won reelection.

During his second term, a depression in Europe spread to the United States, resulting in high unemployment. Scandals also diverted attention from the administration's efforts. Although Grant was never personally implicated in any of the scandals, he did not disassociate himself from the members of his administration who were guilty. His inability to clean up his administration tarnished his reputation in the eyes of the American public. In 1875, he announced that he would not seek a third term. The Republicans nominated Rutherford B. Hayes to be their standard-bearer in the 1876 election.

After his presidency, Grant found himself in economic difficulties and dying of throat cancer. He lost his money in a financial scandal, yet he was determined to provide for his family after his death. After Century Magazine approached him to write articles about his Civil War experiences,

Grant discovered that he enjoyed the process and decided to compile his memoirs. He approached this last battle as he had all others—with grim and dogged determination. His final days were spent on his porch with pencil and paper in hand, wrapped in blankets and in fearsome pain, slowly scrawling out his life's epic tale. He completed the book just days before his death. It was hugely successful and provided for his family's financial security."[23]

---

[23] Miller Center, University of Virginia. http://millercenter.org/president/grant/essays/biography/1

FAMILY

OF

FOUNTAIN SHELTON MAY

Father FOUNTAIN SHELTON MAY PVT-148

Birth	16 Nov 1825	Rockingham County, Virginia[1,2]
Census	1840	Rockingham County, Virginia, age 10-15
Residence	bet 1848 and 54	Augusta County, Virginia
Census	1850	District 2 and A Half, Augusta County, Virginia
Property	21 Apr 1852	51 3/4 acres for $1000 ($19/acre); $200 down; in Turnpike Road near bridge in Christian Creek
Property	Jul 1853	Sheriff's Sale
Birth	12 Aug 1854	son James born, Augusta County, Virginia
Census	3 Jul 1855	Range 22, Sangamon County, Illinois
Residence	Oct 1856	daughter born; Illinois
Residence	Sep 1858	son born; Sullivan County, Missouri
Census	1860	Scottsville, Sullivan County, Missouri
Military	17 Aug 1861	enrolled for 3 years in Co. A, 23rd Regiment of Missouri Volunteers (infantry) as a private; Sullivan County, Missouri
Occupation	17 Aug 1861	a farmer; Sullivan County, Missouri
Military	22 Sep 1861	Mustered into service as a private; Sullivan County, Missouri
Military	6 Apr 1862	Missing in Action; Battle of Shiloh, Pittsburgh, Tennessee
Military	24 May 1862	held prisoner; Montgomery, Alabama
Death	5 Sep 1862	Macon, Bibb County, Georgia
Burial	6 Sep 1862	prob Macon, Ga
Estate		
Misc		was 6' tall, dark complexion, blue eyes, dark hair
Marriage	26 Jul 1848	Staunton, Augusta County, Virginia[3,4]
Father	JACOB MAY-81 (1801-1877)	
Mother	ELIZABETH RAYNES-156 (1806-1872)	

Mother VIRGINIA "Jane" YOUNG-149

Birth	16 Nov 1828	Virginia
Census	1830	Southern District, Augusta County, Virginia
Census	1840	Augusta County, Virginia
Census	1850	District 2 and A Half, Augusta County, Virginia
Census	3 Jul 1855	Sangamon County, Illinois
Residence	1856	from daughter's birth; Illinois
Census	1860	Scottsville, Sullivan County, Missouri
Misc	28 Nov 1862	applied for pension; Sullivan County, Missouri
Misc	7 Jan 1863	Receipt letter from pension office; Sullivan County, Missouri
Misc	18 May 1863	Pension certificate 2167 issued effective Sept 5, 1862 ; Sullivan County, Missouri
Misc	5 Mar 1869	applied for increase of pension; Sullivan County, Missouri
Misc	26 May 1869	Received $8 per month plus $2 per month for 4 children; Sullivan County, Missouri
Census	1870	Bowman Twp., Sullivan County, Missouri
Census	1876	
Census	1880	Bowman Twp., Sullivan County, Missouri
Misc	9 Mar 1886	Pension increased to $12 per month; Sullivan County, Missouri
Census	1900	Sullivan County, Missouri, w/ Jacob and Emily
Will	6 Jul 1900	
Death	10 Jul 1900	6 miles NE of Humphreys, Bowman Twp., Sullivan County, Missouri[5]

---

1. 1850 Census (done in August before his birthday) states age 24, making birthdate 1825; Mueril Moon, granddaughter, says 16 Nov 1825.
2. "Footnotes," digital images, *Ancestry.com* (www.footnote.com : Footnotes image #238095357 7 April 2011), Regimental Descriptive Book.
3. Virginia Young/Fountain May, (28 May 1848), Augusta County, Virginia Marriage Record: 1848-51; Vital Records, Staunton, Virginia.
4. John Vogt & T. William Kethley Jr., *Augusta County Marriages, 1748-1850* (Athens, Georgia: Iberian Publishng Company, n.d.), 138.
5. "A Complete History of Sullivan Co., Missouri" by Crumpacker, pg. 458.

Obit	19 Jul 1900	Sullivan County, Missouri
Burial		Glaze Cemetery, Sullivan County, Missouri
Father	JACOB YOUNG-188 (1805-1846)	
Mother	MARIAH COINER-189 (1808-1863)	

Children

child MAY-2881

Birth	1849	Augusta County, Virginia
Death	1849	Augusta County, Virginia

M *John Ed "DNA" MAY-151

Birth	10 Sep 1850	Augusta County, Virginia
Census	1860	Sullivan County, Missouri
Census	1870	Sullivan County, Missouri
Census	1880	Sullivan County, Missouri
Census	1900	Sullivan County, Missouri
Census	1910	Sullivan County, Missouri
Census	1920	2nd Street, Osgood, Osgood, Sullivan County, Missouri
Death	20 Jun 1926	Sullivan County, Missouri
Obit	21 Jun 1926	
Burial		Campground Cemetery, Osgood, Sullivan County, Missouri[6]
Spouse	Olive J. WILHITE-630 (1851-1938)	
Marriage	24 Oct 1878	Sullivan County, Missouri[7]

M Jacob Henry "Jake DNA" MAY-150

Birth	10 Sep 1850	Augusta County, Virginia
Census	1860	Sullivan County, Missouri
Census	1870	Sullivan County, Missouri
Census	1880	Sullivan County, Missouri
Census	1900	Sullivan County, Missouri
Census	1910	Sullivan County, Missouri
Census	1920	Sullivan County, Missouri
Death	3 Mar 1923	Milan, Sullivan, Missouri
Obit	8 Mar 1923	
Burial		Wilhite Cemetery, Osgood, Sullivan County, Missouri[8]
Spouse	Eliza Mariah WHITE-621 (1855-1923)	
Marriage	7 Mar 1875	Sullivan County, Missouri[9]

F Emma (Emily) Cathern "Hester (Sis)" MAY-152

Birth	29 Dec 1852	Augusta County, Virginia
Census	1860	Sullivan County, Missouri
Census	1870	Sullivan County, Missouri, with family
Residence	1872	schoolteacher; Chillicothe, Livingston, Missouri
Census	1880	Sullivan County, Missouri, with Virginia
Census	1900	Sullivan County, Missouri, with Jacob and Virginia
Death	17 Dec 1939	Chillicothe, Livingston, Missouri[10]
Obit	21 Dec 1939	
Burial		Glaze Cemetery, Sullivan County, Missouri

M James Shelton "Jim" MAY-155

Birth	12 Aug 1854	Augusta County, Virginia
Census	1860	Sullivan County, Missouri
Census	1870	Sullivan County, Missouri

---

6. Sullivan County, Missouri, Campground Cemetery, retrieved from http://ftp.rootsweb.com/pub/usgenweb/mo/sullivan/cemeteries/campground.txt.
7. Complete History of Sullivan County, 1836-1900.
8. www.rootsweb.ancestry.com/~mosulliv/cemeteries/wilhite.html, pg 3.
9. Complete History of Sullivan County 1836-1900.
10. per jjmessersmith notes.

Census	1880	Sullivan County, Missouri
Census	1900	Sullivan County, Missouri
Census	1910	Sullivan County, Missouri
Census	1920	Sullivan County, Missouri
Death	29 Mar 1944	Chillicothe, Livingston, Missouri
Burial		Humphreys Cemetery, Humphreys, Sullivan, Missouri
Obit		
Misc		picture of his home in Dowell packet
Spouse	Nellie Francis (Helen) DEARING-618 (1858-1929)	
Marriage	10 Jan 1875	Milan, Sullivan County, Missouri[11]

F Cornelia Jane "Nealy DNA" MAY-153

Birth	4 Oct 1856	Sangamon County, Illinois
Census	1860	Sullivan County, Missouri
Census	1870	Sullivan County, Missouri
Census	1880	Sullivan County, Missouri
Census	1900	Sullivan County, Missouri
Census	1910	Chillicothe, Livingston, Missouri
Census	1920	Ward 3, Chillicothe, Livingston, Missouri
Census	1930	Chillicothe, Livingston, Missouri
Death	20 Dec 1941	Chillicothe, Livingston, Missouri
Burial		Hutchinson Cemetery, Livingston County, Missouri
Spouse	Robert Newton ANDERSON-642 (1859-1932)	
Marriage	2 Dec 1886	Sullivan County, Missouri[12]

M Samuel Augustus "Gus" MAY-154

Birth	20 Sep 1858	Sullivan County, Missouri
Census	1860	Sullivan County, Missouri
Census	1870	Sullivan County, Missouri
Census	1880	Sullivan County, Missouri
Occupation	1887	teacher; Sullivan County, Missouri
Death	16 Mar 1895	Sullivan County, Missouri
Obit	22 Mar 1895	
Burial		Shatto Cemetery, Milan, Sullivan County, Missouri
Spouse	Elizabeth A. MCCLASKEY-643 (1857-1926)	
Marriage	12 Feb 1880	Sullivan County, Missouri[13]

M WILLIAM GARLAND MAY-137

Birth	11 Jun 1860	Sullivan County, Missouri[14]
Census	1860	Sullivan County, Missouri
Census	1870	Sullivan County, Missouri
Census	1880	Sullivan County, Missouri
Residence	bet 1884 and 86	Barber County, Kansas
Census	1885	Elwood Township, Barber, Kansas
Property	8 Nov 1886	bought SE1/4 SE1/4 of 26-34-13 (40 acres) for $137; Barber County, Kansas
Residence	bet 1888 and 1892	Sullivan County, Missouri
Property	22 Aug 1892	sold NE1/4 of SE 1/4 26-34-13 (40 acres), for $200; Barber County, Kansas
Residence	22 Aug 1892	Sullivan County, Missouri
Residence	bet 1893 and 1910	Barber County, Kansas
Hmstd	1898	NW1/4 NW 1/4 17-34-13 (40 acres); Barber County, Kansas
Residence	19 Sep 1898	Barber County, Kansas
Census	1900	Barber County, Kansas
Occupation	1900	farmer

---

11. Complete History of Sullivan County 1836-1900.
12. Nealey J. May and Robert N. Anderson, (29 November 1886), Book 2: 9; Court House, Milan, Missouri.
13. Complete History of Sullivan County, 1836-1900.
14. Record of Births, Sullivan County, Missouri.

Residence	Dec 1902	bought SE 1/4 18-31-36, 160 acres; Stevens County, Kansas
Census	1905	Harmony Township, Stevens County, Kansas
Census	1910	Stevens County, Kansas
Occupation	1910	farmer
Hmstd	1910	152.95 acres, Homestead Patent # 128062; Stevens Co., Kansas
Census	1915	Harmony Township, Stevens County, Kansas
Misc	31 Mar 1915	post office discontinued; Woodsdale, Stevens, Kansas
Census	1915	Harmony, Stevens, Kansas
Census	1920	Stevens County, Kansas
Occupation	1920	farmer
Census	1925	Moscow, Stevens, Kansas
Misc	Feb 1927	Sold Farm for $8000; Moscow, Stevens, Kansas
Misc	1 Mar 1927	Public Sale of Property; Moscow, Stevens, Kansas
Residence	12 Apr 1928	Two Buttes, Baca, Colorado
Residence	1929	(number on house 405), Wichita, Sedgwick, Kansas
Death	25 May 1930	Wichita, Sedgwick, Kansas age 69[15]
Residence	25 May 1930	405 S. Fern; Wichita, Sedgwick, Kansas
Burial	28 May 1930	Hardtner, Barber, Kansas[16]
Obit	30 May 1930	Hugoton Hermes; Hugoton, Stevens, Kansas
Spouse	SARAH ELIZABETH STERLING-138 (1862-1939)	
Marriage	27 Dec 1883	Sullivan County, Missouri[17]

FAMILY NOTES
Marriage (26 July 1848): Marriage bond posted by Fountain and Jacob May. States that Fountain is the son of Jacob May.

MARRIAGE: Marriage Register record, Augusta Co., Virginia; see also Pension Claim

FATHER NOTES: FOUNTAIN SHELTON MAY PVT-148
Birth (16 November 1825): Regimental Descriptive book gives birthplace
Residence (between 1848 and 54): from marriage date
Census (1850): pg 781; could not read or write
Property (21 April 1852): Fountain bought the land and was selling the lumber to the railroad. He got behind on the payments and the seller foreclosed. He paid $75 1 Sept, 1852 and $25 on 25 Feb, 1853. He was supposed to pay $200 on or before 1 Sept 1852 and $100 by Sept 1853 for total of $1000 ($29,000 in 2010) ($200 equivalent to $5800. So he was obligated to pay $11,600 per year.)
Census (3 July 1855): 3 boys under 10; man 20-30; 1 girl under 10; female 20-30; owned $25 of livestock; was in militia

Sister of Virginia was married in Sangamon County, Illinois

Abraham Lincoln was in area during this time. Shown in 1855 Census in Mechanicsburg, Sangamon County. (Lincoln shown in Springfield in 1850). From 1848-54 he practiced law in this area. Organized Republican Party in 1856. In 1858 ran for Senate.

It is about 875 miles from Staunton, VA to Springfield, IL. Traveling by horse and cart about 10 miles a day, it would take about 88 days.

In 1811 the construction of the Cumberland Road began and by 1852 it was finished. It carried people and goods west with brightly painted stagecoaches pulled by 4 to 6 horses going at least 20 miles an hour.

1806 President Jefferson appointed a board of commissioners to decide upon the exact route through which the extended road would run. The National Road was extended through Columbus, Ohio, Indianapolis, Indian to Vandalia, Illinois at the time it was the capital of Illinois.
According to congressional specifications the Cumberland Road was to be sixty-six feet wide with a surface of stone covered with gravel. Bridges were to be of stone. Grades were to be leveled after the manner of good road construction. The original line from Cumberland to Wheeling was open for traffic in 1818. The first sections constructed were nearly worn out before the western units were completed. The

---

15. Death Certificate, State of Kansas.
16. Ibid.
17. Sarah Sterling/William G. May, (27 December 1883), Sullivan County Marriage Book: p. 211; Sullivan County Courthouse, Milan, Missouri.

route did terminate at Vandalia, IL but never at any time was the National Road a good road from Cumberland to Vandalia. From Terre Haute, Indiana, it was never graded and not entirely cleared of stumps.

Residence (October 1856): from birth of daughter, Cornelia; obit of John Elmer states they lived in Illinois for 2 years

Abraham Lincoln ran for US Senate from Illinois 1854-1858.
Residence (September 1858): from birth of son, Samuel
Census (1860): Age 34; Owned $400 real estate; $208 personal property; could not read or write

There were only 3 towns in Sullivan County in 1862
Military (17 August 1861): Book about Fountain's military service available on Amazon - search Fountain Shelton May.

Private, Company A, 23rd Regiment, Missouri Volunteers. Enrolled at Sullivan County, August 17, 1861 for 3 yrs.; mustered Sept. 22, 1861. Captured April 6, 1862, Pittsburgh, TN (Shiloh), surprise attack at breakfast. Taken to Montgomery, Alabama May 24, 1862. Died at Camp Oglethorpe, Macon, Georgia, Sept. 5, 1862 (Aug. 25, 1862, Sept 21 - several dates are listed but most often Sept. 21; pension application says Sept. 5). Virginia applied for widow's pension #8825 on 28 Nov, 1962. Awarded $8/mo May 9, 1863, beginning Sept. 5, 1862 (certificate 2767); claimed increase under Act of July 25, 1866. Awarded $8/mo. plus $2/child (4 children) beginning July 25, 1866. Received $12/mo until her death 4 May, 1900.
Occupation (17 August 1861): from Regimental Descriptive Book
Military (22 September 1861): Private, Company A, 23rd Regiment, Missouri Volunteers. Enrolled at Sullivan County, August 17, 1861 for 3 yrs.; mustered Sept. 22, 1861. Captured April 6, 1862, Pittsburgh, TN (Shiloh), surprise attack at breakfast. Taken to Montgomery, Alabama May 24, 1862. Died at Camp Oglethorpe, Macon, Georgia, Sept. 5, 1862 (Aug. 25, 1862, Sept 21 - several dates are listed but most often Sept. 21; pension application says Sept. 5). Virginia applied for widow's pension #8825 on 28 Nov, 1962. Awarded $8/mo May 9, 1863, beginning Sept. 5, 1862 (certificate 2767); claimed increase under Act of July 25, 1866. Awarded $8/mo. plus $2/child (4 children) beginning July 25, 1866. Received $12/mo until her death 4 May, 1900.
Military (6 April 1862): In March, 1862, Col. Tindall was ordered with his regiment to St. Louis, where the men were reclothed, and where the Austrian rifle with which they were armed was exchanged for the Springfield rifle. April 1, 1862, they started for Pittsburg Landing, where they arrived on the 4th. Col. Tindall was ordered by Gen. Grant to report to Gen. Prentiss. On the morning of the 6th the regiment, under command of Lieut. Col. Quinn Morton, started out to join the Sixth Division, supposed to be about three miles from the Landing. About two miles out they met large numbers of stragglers from the Eighteenth and Twenty-fifth Missouri Infantry coming toward the Landing in great disorder, who, upon being questioned as to the cause, stated that their regiments had been cut to pieces. An officer of the staff of Gen. Prentiss about this time rode up, and ordered Lieut. Col. Morton to prepare his regiment for action, and with an alacrity and cheerfulness seldom witnessed the regiment prepared to fight its first battle. This was about 9 o'clock in the morning. The rebels opened fire upon them from a battery about 200 yards away, which was kept up without intermission about two hours, at the end of which time they were ordered to change their position in order to engage a large force of the enemy which was pressing upon the center. After a severe fight of some hours, and with serious loss, the enemy was repulsed at 2 P. M. Being out-flanked the regiment changed front, and assisted in repelling frequent charges of the enemy. Soon after 5 P. M. they were surrounded and fired upon from both front and rear. Amid a terrible shower of shot and shell they repulsed the enemy in the rear, and determined to reach the main army which had fallen back to the river, and in the effort to lead his broken forces back Col. Tindall fell, shot through the body, after having done his duty nobly through the day. About 6 P. M. the regiment was met by a large force of rebels, and compelled to surrender. Maj. McCullough is mentioned by Lieut-Col. Quinn Morton (from whose history of this regiment this sketch is in part condensed) as having displayed great coolness and bravery throughout the entire day. This engagement was a severe one for the Twenty-third. Capts. Dunlap, Eobinson and Brown, Adjt. Martin, and Lieuts. Munn and Simms were wounded, thirty private soldiers were killed, about 170 wounded, and 375 taken prisoners.

Company A was raised in part in Sullivan County. Its officers were as follows: Captain, James T. Dunlap, commissioned January 25, 1862, resigned June 27, 1865 ; Lucien Eaton, commissioned July 2, 1863, resigned Special Order No. 204, Department of the Missouri ; T. C. MoNabb, commissioned August 20, 1864, mustered out September 22, 1864. First lieutenant, Ephraim L. Webb, commissioned January 25, 1862, resigned February 2, 1863 ; (A Complete History of Sullivan County, Crumpacker)
Military (24 May 1862): per Memorandum from Prisoner of War Records
Death (5 September 1862): several dates are listed; pension application says Sept. 5; adjuctant general office's receipt of pension states Sept 22; proof exhibit states that the captain of his company testified that he died Sept 5; pension began effective Sept 5

Captured April 6, 1862, Pittsburg, TN (Shiloh); surprise attack at breakfast. Taken to Montgomery, Alabama on May 24, 1862; Died at Macon, Georgia on Sept 5, 1862; died of chronic diarrhea and corroborated leg at Camp Oglethorpe, Macon, Georgia. (from military and pension records)

Between 1865 and 1868 the bodies of burials at Camp Oglethorpe were moved and reburied in the Andersonville National Cemetery. They are buried there in Section B.

There is a good chance he was buried in Rose Hill cemetery. The site of the camp is now a rail road switching yard. There are about 100 unknown confederates buried there, I also think several Union soldiers are buried there. The old cemetery on lower 7th Street was cut by

7th Street in the 1960's and some graves were removed, but I don't know where, probably Rose Hill cemetery which is on River Side Drive. This cemetery is owned by the City of Macon. The Macon historical society may be able to help you, phone # 478-742-5084.
Burial (6 September 1862): There is a G(?)P May and O.H.P. May buried in Soldier's Square at Rose Hill Cemetery, Macon, Ga. This is where the burials from Oglethorpe were supposed re-located.
Estate: August 1874. Petition for discharge of Estate of Fountain May filed by James Beatty, Admr., 11 Jul 1870. Mentions widow but no name.
Misc: per regimental descriptive book, civil war
General: PARENTS: Marriage bond posted by Fountain and Jacob May. States that Fountain is the son of Jacob May. Mother not proven.

Capt. James T. Dunlap and Mariah Young knew Fountain and Virginia since 1845. Mariah is Virginia's mother. Capt. Dunlap may be the husband of Cynthia, Virginia's sister.

Notes attached to John E. May's obit: My grandfather Fountain May was in Company I, 14 Mo. Inf., was captured at Battle of Shiloh, was in Andersonville prison for duration of war. All was affected with scurvy and floody flux, had to fight for and steal their medicine.

MOTHER NOTES: VIRGINIA YOUNG-149
Birth (16 November 1828): BIRTH: Death records, from "A Complete History of Sullivan Co., Missouri," Crumpacker
Census (3 July 1855): Sister of Virginia was married in Sangamon County, Illinois
Census (1860): Owned $400 real estate; $208 personal property
Misc (28 November 1862): Act of July 14, 1862
Misc (18 May 1863): $8 per month
Misc (5 March 1869): Under the Act of July 25, 1866
Misc (26 May 1869): effective 25 July 1866; she probably received about $360 in arrears
Census (1870): Owned $308 of real estate; $800 personal property
Will (6 July 1900): I, Virginia May, being of sound mind, do hereby give and bequeath to Emma Catharine May, all of my personal property wherever found, and all crops growing on any land and now to me in possession, except my bed and bedding, cattle, hogs, which is to be equally distributed among the heirs, and be it understood that the aforesaid Emma Catharine May is to be furnished out of the Estate with provisions for one year. Virginia May (signed with X). Witnesses J. M. Sullivan, Sarah Henry. (Book B, page 445, Will Record, Sullivan County, Missouri)

Have copy of original
Death (10 July 1900): Died of jaundice per obituary

DEATH: Death records, from "A Complete History of Sullivan Co., Missouri," Crumpacker

DIED
Virginia May, mother of Jacob, John and James May, of this county, and Wm. May, of Kansas, died at her home in Bowman Township Tuesday after a long illness. The funeral took place Wednesday afternoon. (12 July 1900, Sullivan County Library, Milan, Missouri)

Obit (19 July 1900): OBITUARY
Mrs. Virginia May died July 10, 1900, at her home six miles northeast of Humphreys. Virginia Young was born November 16, 1828, in West Virginia, where she grew to womanhood and was married to Fountain May 1849. To this union was born eight children, the first died in infancy, Jacob and John, twins, and James May, all prosperous farmers of Sullivan County. Augustus May, who met his death by accident in a factory in Milan where he was laboring to support a loving wife and affectionate children; Emily C. May, a dutiful daughter who gave up this world's pleasures and youthful companions and devoted her life to her mother during the 38 years of widowhood. In 1862 her father left wife and children and pleasures of home for love of country and joined the 28th Mo. Infantry and was taken prisoner in the first day's fight on Shiloh's blood field, and died in the Macon Georgia prison September 5, 1862. Since then (Sis as everybody calls her) has been the ever faithful, never murmuring, always willing child; Cornelia Anderson whose whereabouts are not known at present writing, and William G. May, of Kansas, who did not get here until death had claimed its own.
Mrs. May died with that dread disease jaundice. Everything was done that medicine and loving hands, could do, but God said "come unto me and I will give you rest." Mrs. May professed religion about 30 years ago at the old Wilhite school house on a puncheon seat with four legs in it and that was a good kind for she has lived so that the world could see that the bible is true, "By their works ye shall know them". She was surrounded by her children and grand children and one sister Mrs. Thomas Dunlap, who lives near Milan, and a host of sorrowing friends to see the last light go out on earth to light in heaven.

The funeral was preached at the house by Rev. J.S. Todd, of Gault. The remains was followed by a large concourse of sorrowing relatives and friends, and laid to rest in the Glaze grave yard to wait the resurrection morn.
"Asleep in Jesus, blessed sleep, From which none ever wakes to weep." M.E. Henly.

This Obituary was found in the obituary records for Sullivan County, Missouri. I believe the newspaper it was found in was the Trenton Republic Newspaper.
Burial: BURIAL: Glaze Cemetery near Humphreys, Mo. with infant, daughter of N.W. and D.E.

General: In her request for a pension, Capt. James T. Dunlap and Mariah Young knew her since 1845. Mariah is Virginia's mother. Capt. Dunlap is the husband of Cynthia, Virginia's sister.

1900 Census - Sullivan Co., Missouri, age 71
1880 Census - Sullivan Co., Missouri, age 57
1870 Census - Sullivan Co., Missouri, age 48
1860 Census - Sullivan Co., Missouri, age 31
1850 Census - Augusta Co., Virginia, age 22

James S. (and wife Nellie), John E. (and wife Olive) are buried at Humphreys cemetery.
Jacob H. (and wife Eliza) are buried at Wilhite Cemetery near Osgood, Mo.
Samuel buried at Shatto Cemetery, Sullivan Co., Mo.
William Garland, Jr. buried at City Cemetery, Hartner, Ks.

Any child going to school under 6 years of age, will have to stop by the 30th, and any over 20 and under 21 must stop too or pay. This is the new constitution. (Sullivan Standard, 1875)

The procession of Ku Klux will appear on our streets tomorrow afternoon at 5:30 o'clock. Remain in town and see them. (Sullivan Standard, 4 June 1875)

Wild turkeys are plentiful in our district (Sullivan Standard, 4 June 1875)

The Ku Klux, in full and grotesque uniform, appeared on horseback, about 4 o'clock and marched through our principal streets. On the grounds a large tent was stretched where many passed away the afternoon in dancing. At night there was a grand display of fireworks from the top of the bank. Only a few drunks were on the street. (4 July 1875)

Prairie chickens were never more plentiful (23 Nov 1877)

Anderson's Circus exhibits at Lindley, Browning and Wintersville this week. (2 Aug 1878)

A little mound near the Hodge Mill has been opened and a half dozen partly decayed skeletons have been unearthed. They belonged to human beings and were the largest ever seen in this country. It was thought at first that they belonged to the race of Indians which last inhabited this section but upon closer examination they were found to be entirely too large. Just to what race of beings they did belong cannot be determined, but one thing is certain "there were giants in those days". A portion of these skeletons can be seen at D. E. Shearers. (19 April 1878)

The census showed Sullivan County had a population of 19,000. (Feb 27, 1891)

The veteran champion of Women's Rights, Susan B. Anthony, will deliver her great lecture "Woman wants bread not the ballot," at Tripp's Opera House, Wednesday evening, April 15, 1885. Admission 50 cents, no extra charge for reserved seats. p407

http://www.progenealogists.com/palproject/pa/1729mort.htm

PARENTS

AND

SIBLINGS

OF

FOUNTAIN SHELTON MAY

Father	JACOB MAY-81	
Birth	abt Feb 1801	Rockingham County, Virginia
Census	1830	
Census	1840	Rockingham County, Virginia, age 40-50
Census	1850	District 2 and A Half, Augusta County, Virginia, age 50
Occupation	1850	miller; District 2 and A Half, Augusta County, Virginia
Census	1870	Second Creek, Monroe Co., West Virginia
Occupation	1870	miller; Monroe Co., West Virginia
Death	3 Jul 1877	Second Creek, Monroe, West Virginia
Marriage	3 Jan 1825	Rockingham County, Virginia[1,2]
Father	ADAM MAY-2300 (1769-1834)	
Mother	ELIZABETH BOTT-2301 (1774-1851)	
Other spouse	unknown MAY-7261 (-)	
Marriage	aft 1872	

Mother	ELIZABETH RAYNES-156	
Birth	19 Jun 1806	Botetourt County, Virginia
Census	1830	
Census	1840	Rockingham County, Virginia, age 30-40
Census	1850	District 2 and A Half, Augusta County, Virginia
Census	1870	Second Creek, Monroe Co., West Virginia, age 62
Death	28 Aug 1872	Monroe County, West Virginia
Father	Lawrence RAYNES-2312 (1760-1837)	
Mother	Mary KNIGHT-4092 (1766-1843)	

Children

M	Albert F. MAY-157	
Birth	May 1824	Virginia
Census	1850	District 2 and A Half, Augusta County, Virginia
Census	1860	District 3, Rockbridge County, Virginia
Census	1870	Amsterdam, Botetourt, Virginia
Occupation	1870	Miller; Amsterdam, Botetourt, Virginia
Census	1880	Big Lick, Roanoke, Virginia
Census	1900	Ward 3, Roanoke, Roanoke, Virginia
Death	aft 1900	possibly Roanoke, Virginia
Military		
Spouse	Mary F. BREEDAN-3378 (1836-)	
Marriage	28 Jul 1853	Rockingham County, Virginia

M	FOUNTAIN SHELTON MAY PVT-148	
Birth	16 Nov 1825	Rockingham County, Virginia[3,4]
Census	1840	Rockingham County, Virginia, age 10-15
Residence	bet 1848 and 54	Augusta County, Virginia
Census	1850	District 2 and A Half, Augusta County, Virginia
Property	21 Apr 1852	51 3/4 acres for $1000 ($19/acre); $200 down; in Turnpike Road near bridge in Christian Creek
Property	Jul 1853	Sheriff's Sale
Birth	12 Aug 1854	son James born, Augusta County, Virginia
Census	3 Jul 1855	Range 22, Sangamon County, Illinois
Residence	Oct 1856	daughter born; Illinois
Residence	Sep 1858	son born; Sullivan County, Missouri

---

1. Marriage Bond, dated 3 Jan. 1825.
2. John Vogt & T. William Kethley Jr., *Virginia Historic Marriage Register: Rockingham County Marriages, 1778-1850* (Athens, Georgia: n.p., 1984), 151.
3. 1850 Census (done in August before his birthday) states age 24, making birthdate 1825; Mueril Moon, granddaughter, says 16 Nov 1825.
4. "Footnotes," digital images, *Ancestry.com* (www.footnote.com : Footnotes image #238095357 7 April 2011), Regimental Descriptive Book.

	Census	1860	Scottsville, Sullivan County, Missouri
	Military	17 Aug 1861	enrolled for 3 years in Co. A, 23rd Regiment of Missouri Volunteers (infantry) as a private; Sullivan County, Missouri
	Occupation	17 Aug 1861	a farmer; Sullivan County, Missouri
	Military	22 Sep 1861	Mustered into service as a private; Sullivan County, Missouri
	Military	6 Apr 1862	Missing in Action; Battle of Shiloh, Pittsburgh, Tennessee
	Military	24 May 1862	held prisoner; Montgomery, Alabama
	Death	5 Sep 1862	Macon, Bibb County, Georgia
	Burial	6 Sep 1862	prob Macon, Ga
	Estate		
	Misc		was 6' tall, dark complexion, blue eyes, dark hair
	Spouse		VIRGINIA YOUNG-149 (1828-1900)
	Marriage	26 Jul 1848	Staunton, Augusta County, Virginia[5,6]
M	**Eleazer "Eli" MAY-158**		
	Birth	Jan 1828	Rockingham County, Virginia
	Census	1850	District 2 and A Half, Augusta County, Virginia
	Census	1870	Sweet Springs, Monroe, West Virginia
	Census	1900	Covington, Alleghany, Virginia
	Death	13 Apr 1904	Smith City, Mt. Pleasant, Alleghany, Virginia
	Spouse		Frances Jane MCCLELLAND-3377 (1844-)
	Marriage	19 Oct 1863	Rockbridge Co., Virginia
F	**Mary Elizabeth MAY-159**		
	Birth	1830	Virginia
	Census	1850	District 2 and A Half, Augusta County, Virginia
	Death	bef 1860	
	Spouse		George H. YOUNG-190 (1832-1900)
	Marriage	22 Mar 1853	Augusta County, Virginia
M	**Garland MAY-161**		
	Birth	1833	Virginia
	Census	1850	District 2 and A Half, Augusta County, Virginia
	Census	1860	Brandy City, Sierra, California
	Military	1 Jul 1863	registration; Brittons, California
	Census	1880	Mineral Park, Mohave, Arizona
	Misc	1890	voter registration; San Joaquin, California
	Death	aft 1890	prob California
F	**Mahala MAY-162**		
	Birth	1835	Virginia
	Census	1850	District 2 and A Half, Augusta County, Virginia
M	**William H. H. MAY-163**		
	Birth	1837	Rockingham County, Virginia
	Census	1850	District 2 and A Half, Augusta County, Virginia
	Military	28 Sep 1861	Pvt (Confederate); Company G, 5 Reg't Virginia Infantry, Staunton, Augusta, Virginia
	Military	3 Oct 1862	promoted to 5 Sgt
	Military	3 May 1863	wounded
	Military	Sep 1864	4 Sgt
	Military	31 Oct 1864	reduced to private; transferred from Co. G to H
	Military	21 Mar 1865	takes oath - transferred to Scottsville, Sullivan County, Missouri
M	**Annanias MAY-164**		
	Birth	1840	Rockingham County, Virginia
	Census	1850	District 2 and A Half, Augusta County, Virginia

---

5. Virginia Young/Fountain May, (28 May 1848), Augusta County, Virginia Marriage Record: 1848-51; Vital Records, Staunton, Virginia.
6. John Vogt & T. William Kethley Jr., *Augusta County Marriages, 1748-1850* (Athens, Georgia: Iberian Publishng Company, n.d.), 138.

	Census	1870	Second Creek, Monroe Co., West Virginia
	Census	1880	Blacksburg, Montgomery, Virginia
	Census	1910	Salem Ward 1, Roanoke, Virginia
	Death	aft 1910	
	Spouse	Mary Emma POBST-3380 (1847-1910)	
	Marriage	31 Jul 1867	Roanoke County, Virginia
F	**Ann MAY-165**		
	Birth	1840	Rockingham County, Virginia
	Census	1850	District 2 and A Half, Augusta County, Virginia
	Census	1870	Second Creek, Monroe Co., West Virginia
	Census	1880	Peterstown, Monroe, West Virginia
	Census	1900	Second Creek, Monroe Co., West Virginia
	Death	22 Mar 1926	Greenbriar County, West Virginia
	Spouse	Robert P. VAUGHN-3379 (1826-)	
	Marriage	14 Jul 1874	Monroe County, West Virginia
F	**Martha Hester MAY-166**		
	Birth	Feb 1842	Virginia
	Census	1850	District 2 and A Half, Augusta County, Virginia
	Census	1870	Second Creek, Monroe Co., West Virginia
	Census	1880	Blue Sulphur, Greenbriar County, West Virginia
F	**Nancy MAY-167**		
	Birth	Jun 1846	Virginia
	Census	1850	District 2 and A Half, Augusta County, Virginia
	Census	1870	Second Creek, Monroe Co., West Virginia
	Census	1880	Blue Sulphur, Greenbriar County, West Virginia
M	**Zachary Taylor MAY-168**		
	Birth	Jun 1849	Virginia
	Census	1850	District 2 and A Half, Augusta County, Virginia
	Census	1870	Second Creek, Monroe Co., West Virginia
	Occupation	1880	Miller; Greenbriar County, West Virginia
	Census	1880	Blue Sulphur, Greenbriar County, West Virginia, age 26
	Census	1910	Blue Sulphur, Greenbriar County, West Virginia, age 60
	Census	1920	Blue Sulphur, Greenbriar County, West Virginia
	Death	22 Apr 1927	Asbury, Greenbriar, West Virginia
	Burial	23 Apr 1927	Emmanuel Methodist Church Cemetery, Asbury, Greenbriar, West Virginia
	Spouse	Capitola Eugenia PARRENT-3381 (1859-1923)	
	Marriage	21 Oct 1880	Gallia County, Ohio

FAMILY NOTES
Marriage (3 January 1825): Marriage Bond states Elizabeth is daughter of Lawrence Raines

from Joseph Messersmith, 11479 Primrose Ln., Rockville, VA 23146

Marriage Bond Book, 1778-1816, Clerk's Office, Rockingham County, VA

FATHER NOTES: JACOB MAY-81
Birth (about February 1801): Check Frieden's Church register for birth registration
Census (1830): Two Jacob May families in Rockingham in 1830 but both have too many children
Census (1840): with wife 30-39, and 6 sons, 3 daughters
Census (1850): Listed with family
Occupation (1850): pg 707
Census (1870): Listed with children and wife, Elizabeth
Death (3 July 1877): Have copy of record; Elizabeth died in Monroe, WV also and 1870 census has correct children listed.

The three youngest children were in Greenbriar Co., WV in 1880

General: Link to Adam May confirmed by DNA match to Y-DNA May Family Reconstruction Project, Testee 2, Family 25

Joseph J. Messersmith, Jr. Notes: Jacob May's link to Adam May is based several pieces of circumstantial evidence which I will listed below.
1. Several years on the Rockingham County personal property tax lists, Jacob's name was listed "Jacob May (of Adam)", meaning Jacob, son of Adam.
2. Jacob lived in the same area of Rockingham County as his father and other brothers.
3. Jacob married Elizabeth Raines, daughter of Lawrence Raines. Nancy Raines, also a daughter of Lawrence Raines, married Adam May, Jr. It was common in those days for siblings to marry siblings. The Raineses and Mays lived near each other in the Port Republic area of Rockingham County.
4. Adam May, Jr. is a known son of Adam May, Sr. since his birth is recorded in the Friedens Church register.
 (jjmessersmith@comcast.net) 11/4/2005

MOTHER NOTES: ELIZABETH RAYNES-156
Birth (19 June 1806): Calculated from death date
Death (28 August 1872): per West Virginia death index, 1853-1973, FHL film #589915

KNOW all men by these presents, that we Jacob May and Lawrence Raines are held and firmly bound unto His Excellency, James Pleasants Esquire, Governor of Virginia, and his Successors for the use of the Commonwealth, in Sum the of One Hundred and Fifty Dollars to which payment well and truly to be made we bind ourselves, our heirs, executors and administrators jointly and severally, firmly by these presents Sealed and dated this 3rd day of Jany 1825 in the 49 year of the Commonwealth.

The Condition of the above obligation is such, that whereas a marriage is shortly intended to be solemnized between the above bound Jacob May and Elizabeth Raines the Daughter of Lawrence Raines of Rockingham County. if therefore there shall be no lawful cause to obstruct the said marriage, then the above obligation to be void: otherwise, to remain in full force and virtue.

Signed, Sealed and delivered in the Presence of

L. W. Gambill

Jacob May {L.S.}
Lawrence (his mark) Raines {L.S.}

Ger F.
7-9-1940

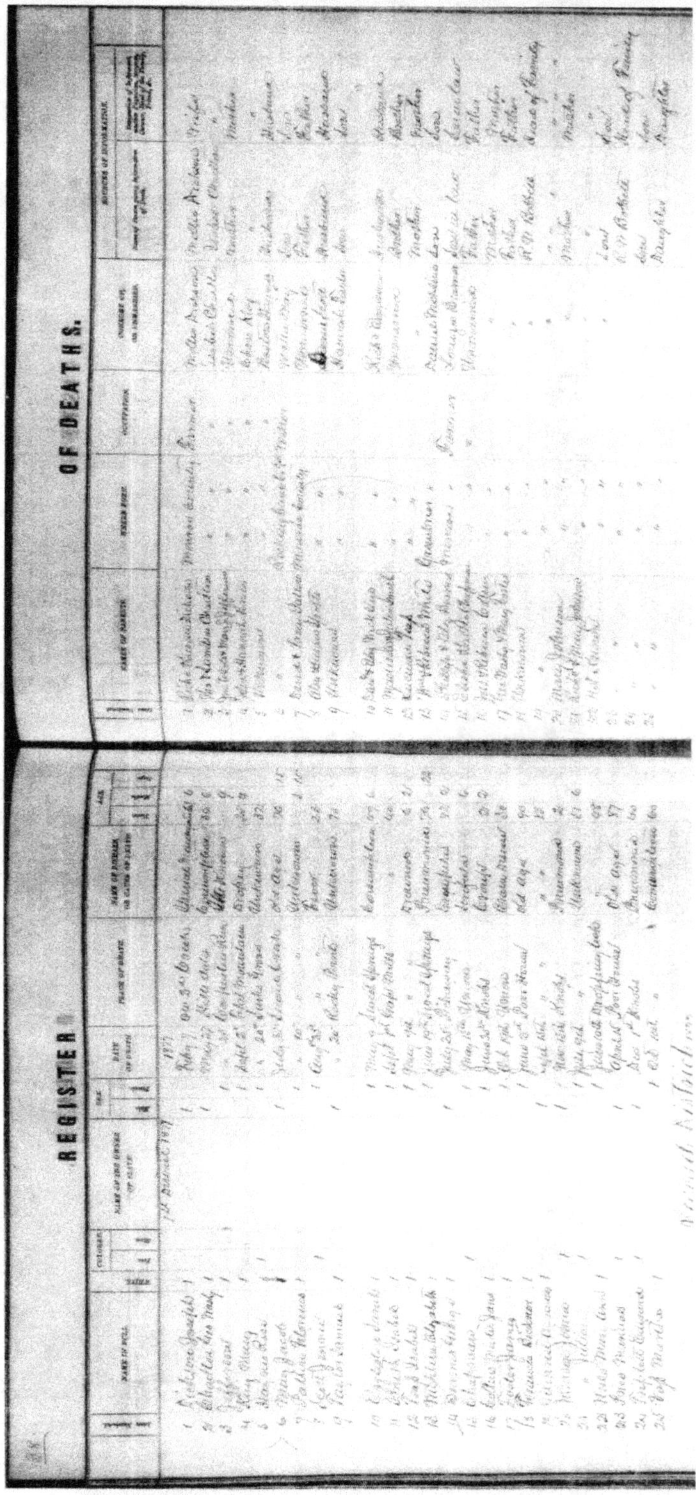
REGISTER OF DEATHS.

West Virginia Death Records
West Virginia Archives

www.wvculture.org

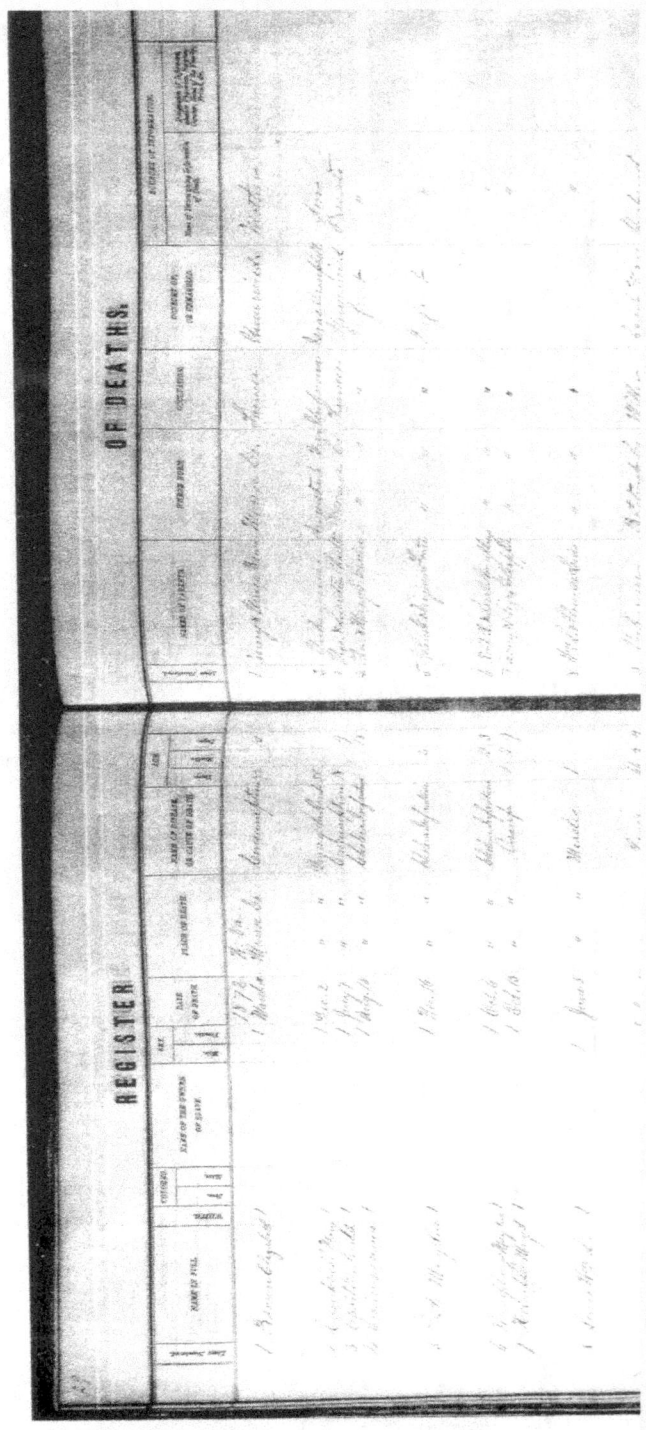

ANCESTORS

OF

FOUNTAIN SHELTON MAY

Lineage of Fountain Shelton May

......10 Fountain Shelton May b: 16 Nov 1825 Rockingham Co VA d: 5 Sept 1862 Macon GA
............+Virginia Young b: 16 Nov 1828 VA d: 10 Jul 1900 Sullivan Co MO

..........9 Jacob May b: Feb 1801 VA d: 3 Jul 1877 W VA
................+Elizabeth Raines b: 19 Jun 1806 VA d: 28 Aug 1872 W VA

............8 Adam May b: 23 Oct 1769 Montgomery Co PA d: abt 1835 Rockingham Co VA
................+Elizabeth Bott b: abt 1774 MD m: aft 11 Nov 1791 Augusta Co VA

...............7 Christian May b: abt 1735 d: aft 1810
...................+Anna Maria (?) d: bet 1769-1774

....................6 Johann Freidrich Mey b: 13 Nov 1711 Alsenz, Pfalz, Germany
.... +Anna Catharina Lenneg?
                       m: 14 Feb 1730 Meisenheim Schlosskirche, Germany

...........................5 Johannes Mey b: 15 Apr 1689 Alsenz, Pfalz, Germany
                            d 1750 Alsenz, Pfalz, Germany
.............................+Elisabetha Catharina Beyer b: Odernheim Germany
                            m: 27 Jan 1711 Alsenz, Pfalz, Germany

..................................4 Johannes Mey
                              b: 24 Dec 1638 Callbach, Rheinland, Pfalz, Germany
                              d: 25 Jan 1720 Alsenz, Rheinland Pfalz, Germany
......................................+Margaretha Lauers
                              b: 23 Mar 1643 Niedermoschel, Rheinland Pfalz, Germany
                              m: 7 Mar 1665 Alsenz, Pfalz, Germany
                              d: 23 Apr 1707 Alsenz, Rheinland Pfalz, Germany

....3 Heinrich Mey b: 4 Nov 1602 Callbach, Pfalz, Germany
                              d: 7 Jan 1671 Callbach, Pfalz, Germany
....+Appollonia (?) b: abt Feb 1596
                              d: 27 Mar 1674 Callbach or Meisenheim, Pfalz, Germany

....2 Conradt Mey b: 6 Sept 1567 Callbach, Pfalz, Germany
                              d: 10 Dec 1614 Callbach, Pfalz, Germany
....+Maria (?)

....1 Hans Peter Mey
                              b: abt 1540 Callbach, Pfalz, Germany
....+Christina (?)

--Confirmed by DNA match to Y-DNA May Family Reconstruction Project Testee 2, Family 25

Y-DNA REPORT (FTDNA)

Family 189. The May family, ancestors of Edward L. May, son of Hallie May, grandson of Burney May, g-grandson of William Garland May, g-g-grandson of **Fountain Shelton May,** g-g-g-grandson of Jacob May.

Family 189 matches 36/37 to Family 25 (testee 2); 35/37 to Family 211; 33/37 to Family 25 (testee 1); and 24/25 to Family 31. Researcher: Flora McCarty

FAMILY 15: The MAY family of Hans Peter Mey, born c1540 in Germany. Researcher: John Greenley MAY

FAMILY 25 (testee 1): The May family of Albert Osborn (1818-1904) who was apparently an illegitimate son of a Mr. May in Floyd County, Kentucky, probably of the Niederhausen, Germany line of the May family. If so, this line should match that of Family 15. This family is 23/25 to Family 15 and 23/25 to Family 31. Researcher: Donald Lewis Osborn

FAMILY 25 (testee 2): A test was ordered of a descendant of REUBEN MAY (1800-1840) who married Sally Allen (This is the Reuben that the researcher thinks was father of Don's great-grandfather Albert Osborn). Researcher: Donald Lewis Osborn.

FAMILY 31: The May family descendents of Adam MAY, b 1765-70 in PA, d. 1834-40 in Rockingham Co., VA. He m.Elizabeth BOTT in 1791 in Augusta Co., VA. She was b. c1770 in MD, d. aft 1850 in Port Republic, Rockingham Co., VA. Researcher: Harrison May

FAMILY 211: The May ancestors of James A. Maye. Researcher: Kathy Rosa

A **Y** chromosome **DNA** test (**Y-DNA** test) is a genealogical **DNA** test which is used to explore a man's patrilineal or direct father's-line ancestry. The **Y** chromosome, like the patrilineal surname, passes down virtually unchanged from father to son.

Matches for DNA are based on how many alleles (or markers) match between two persons tested. Thus a 24/25 match means that out of 25 alleles tested, 24 match - or 33/37 means that out of 37 alleles tested, 33 match. Generally, the more alleles tested, the more accurate the test is. Therefore the strongest match of these families to **Family 189** is Family 25 (testee 2). The Reuben May referenced is a grandson of Adam May, grandfather of Fountain Shelton May.

Information about the matching families is dependent on what is entered by the researcher. Matches were only made between persons testing in the FTDNA company and will not reflect matches in Ancestry, 23 & Me or other companies without submitting tests in those companies.

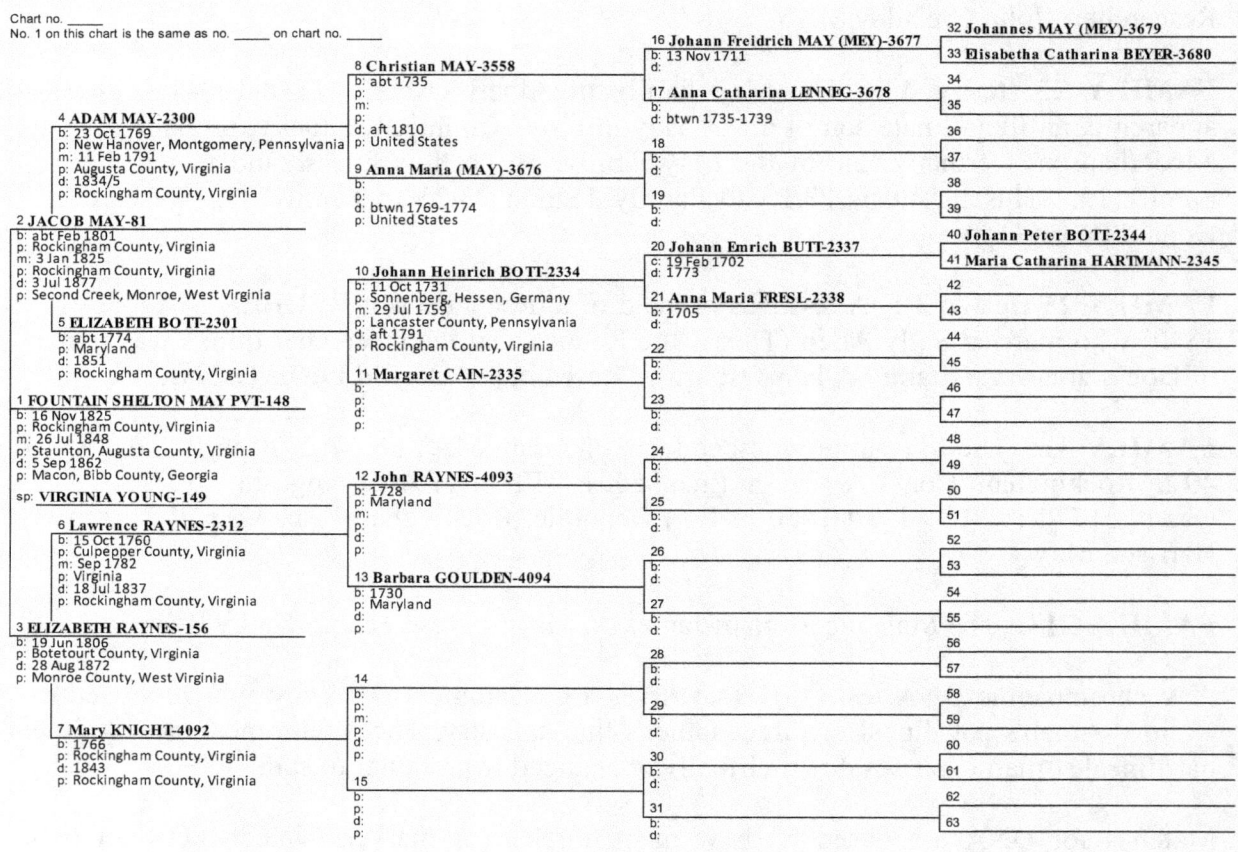

Father	ADAM MAY-2300	
Birth	23 Oct 1769	New Hanover, Montgomery, Pennsylvania
Baptism	28 Jan 1770	New Hanover, Montgomery, Pennsylvania
Misc	1778	created from Augusta County; Rockingham County, Virginia
Misc	10 Sep 1784	created from Philadelphia County; Montgomery County, Pennsylvania
Residence	1792	Rockingham County, Virginia
Misc	1801	Jacob born; Rockingham County, Virginia
Census	1810	New Haven, Rockingham, Virginia
Census	1820	Rockingham County, Virginia
Census	1830	Rockingham County, Virginia
Death	1834/5	Rockingham County, Virginia
Marriage	11 Feb 1791	bond date, Augusta County, Virginia[1]
Father	Christian MAY-3558 (1735-1810)	
Mother	Anna Maria (MAY)-3676 (-)	

Mother	ELIZABETH BOTT-2301	
Birth	abt 1774	Maryland
Census	1830	
Census	1840	Rockingham County, Virginia
Death	1851	Rockingham County, Virginia
Father	Johann Heinrich BOTT-2334 (1731-1791)	
Mother	Margaret CAIN-2335 (-)	

Children

F	Mary Agathy "Polly" MAY-2302	
Birth	11 Feb 1792	Rockingham County, Virginia
Death	8 Sep 1866	Augusta County, Virginia
Burial	9 Sep 1866	Melanchthon Chapel Cemetery, Augusta County, Virginia
Spouse	David CRICKENBERGER-3410 (1783-1855)	
Marriage	13 Feb 1810	Rockingham County, Virginia

M	John MAY-2303	
Birth	abt 1793	Rockingham County, Virginia
Death	aft 1860	
Spouse	Catherine EUTSLER-3411 (1782-1860)	
Marriage	27 Mar 1820	Rockingham County, Virginia

F	Savilla MAY-2304	
Birth	1797	Rockingham County, Virginia
Death	bef 15 Jun 1835	Rockingham County, Virginia

M	Adam MAY Jr.-2305	
Birth	1 May 1798	Rockingham County, Virginia
Chr	2 Dec 1798	Rockingham County, Virginia
Military	1813	
Death	14 Jun 1874	Rockingham County, Virginia
Burial	15 Jun 1874	Central Cemetery, Port Republic, Rockingham County, Virginia
Spouse	Nancy RAYNES-3409 (1800-1845)	
Marriage	25 Jun 1821	Rockingham County, Virginia

M	JACOB MAY-81	
Birth	abt Feb 1801	Rockingham County, Virginia
Census	1830	
Census	1840	Rockingham County, Virginia, age 40-50
Census	1850	District 2 and A Half, Augusta County, Virginia, age 50
Occupation	1850	miller; District 2 and A Half, Augusta County, Virginia
Census	1870	Second Creek, Monroe Co., West Virginia
Occupation	1870	miller; Monroe Co., West Virginia
Death	3 Jul 1877	Second Creek, Monroe, West Virginia
Spouse	unknown MAY-7261 (-)	

---

1. Augusta County, Virginia, marriage bond (11 February 1791); Augusta County Courthouse, Staunton.

	Marriage	aft 1872	
	Spouse	ELIZABETH RAYNES-156 (1806-1872)	
	Marriage	3 Jan 1825	Rockingham County, Virginia[2,3]
F	**Elizabeth MAY-3412**		
	Birth	2 Sep 1801	Rockingham County, Virginia
	Death	aft 1850	
	Spouse	John BLAKELY-3413 (1779-)	
	Marriage	4 Mar 1820	Rockingham County, Virginia
M	**Henry MAY-2306**		
	Birth	15 Feb 1802	Rockingham County, Virginia
	Chr	20 Jun 1802	Rockingham County, Virginia
	Death	24 Jun 1884	
	Spouse	Elizabeth GREENWOOD-3414 (1804-)	
	Marriage	24 Mar 1828	Rockingham County, Virginia
M	**Daniel Adam MAY-2307**		
	Birth	8 Dec 1805	Rockingham County, Virginia
	Death	1 Oct 1865	Mt. Crawford, Rockingham Co., Virginia
	Burial	2 Oct 1865	Northern Methodist Cemetery, Mt. Crawford, Rockingham County, Virginia
	Spouse	Elizabeth BATEMAN-3415 (1815-)	
	Marriage	6 Mar 1832	Rockingham County, Virginia
F	**Christina MAY-2308**		
	Birth	11 Mar 1808	Rockingham County, Virginia
	Chr	16 Apr 1809	Rockingham County, Virginia
	Death	16 Feb 1880	Rockingham County, Virginia
F	**Gertrude Catherine MAY-2309**		
	Birth	4 Jul 1812	Rockingham County, Virginia
	Chr	17 Oct 1812	Rockingham County, Virginia
	Census	1880	widowed, Stone Wall, Rockingham, Virginia
	Burial	Jul 1889	Mill Creek Church of the Brethren Cemetery, Port Republic, Rockingham County, Virginia
	Death	Jul 1889	Rockingham County, Virginia
	Spouse	unknown UNKNOWN-7274 (-)	
F	**Sarah MAY-2310**		
	Birth	11 Aug 1814	Rockingham County, Virginia
	Chr	18 Jun 1815	Rockingham County, Virginia
	Death	bef 1889	
M	**Samuel MAY-2311**		
	Birth	26 Nov 1816	Rockingham County, Virginia
	Chr	11 May 1817	Rockingham County, Virginia
	Death	1 Jun 1901	Berkeley Co., West Virginia
	Spouse	Mary SIPE-2316 (-)	
	Marriage	3 Feb 1842	Rockingham County, Virginia[4]

FAMILY NOTES
Marriage (11 February 1791): Have copy.

Know all men by these presents that we Adam May &Christian Huffman are held and firmly bound unto his Excellence of Beverly Randolph e.g. Governor of Virginia and his successors in the sum of fifty pounds current money % the payment whereof well and truly to be made. We do bind ourselves our heirs, exrs & admrs jointly and severally firmly by these present seals with our seals this 11th day of February 1791 in the 15th year of the Commonwealth.
The conditions of the above obligation is such that whereas there is a marriage shortly intended to be solemnized between the above bound

---

2. Marriage Bond, dated 3 Jan. 1825.
3. John Vogt & T. William Kethley Jr., *Virginia Historic Marriage Register: Rockingham County Marriages, 1778-1850* (Athens, Georgia: n.p., 1984), 151.
4. Virginia Historic Marriage Registry, Rockingham County Marriages, 1778-1850; John Vogt & T. William Kethley, Jr., Athens, Georgia 1984.

Adam May & Elizabeth Butt, daughter of Henry Butt of Augusta. If therefore there shall be no lawful cause to obstruct the said marriage then obligation is to be void otherwise to remain in full force.
2 Witnesses (cannot read names)

This marriage record was originally published in "Chronicles of the Scotch-Irish Settlement in Virginia, 1745-1800". Extracted from the Original Court Records of Augusta County by Lyman Chalkley.

FATHER NOTES: ADAM MAY-2300
Birth (23 October 1769): Have copy - New Hanover Evangelical Lutheran Church
Residence (1792): per child's birth
General: Jacob May's link to Adam May is based several pieces of circumstantial evidence which I will listed below.
1. Several years on the Rockingham County personal property tax lists, Jacob's name was listed "Jacob May (of Adam)", meaning Jacob, son of Adam.
2. Jacob lived in the same area of Rockingham County as his father and other brothers.
3. Jacob married Elizabeth Raines, daughter of Lawrence Raines. Nancy Raines, also a daughter of Lawrence Raines, married Adam May, Jr. It was common in those days for siblings to marry siblings. The Raineses and Mays lived near each other in the Port Republic area of Rockingham County.
4. Adam May, Jr. is a known son of Adam May, Sr. since his birth is recorded in the Friedens Church register.
Joseph J. Messersmith, Jr. (jjmessersmith@comcast.net) 11/4/2005

from Joseph Messersmith, 11479 Primrose Ln., Rockville, VA 23146

Not on list of Large Landowners of Rockingham County in the year 1789 (Genweb)

Ancestors of Adam May per Messersmith

MOTHER NOTES: ELIZABETH BOTT-2301
Birth (about 1774): If Elizabeth was born in Maryland, as it states on the 1850 census, then she was born as Henry emigrated to Virginia from Pennsylvania
Census (1840): With 2 females, 20-29 (Sarah and Gertrude?); 1 female, 10-14; 1 male, 20-29 (Samuel?)
General: Marriage bond record states bride is daughter of Henry Bott, who consents.

Posted by: Buddy Hanna Date: June 21, 1998 at 12:45:54
Elizabeth was born in Maryland in the mid 1770s. She Married Adam May of Penn. and they moved to Rockingham Co., Va. They had at least 2 children, Adam and Elizabeth. Elizabeth was born in 1794 and Married John Blakely (Blakeley) in Rockingham Co., Va. They later moved to Augusta Co., Va.

Posted by: Susan Mullins Date: March 02, 2000 at 14:12:17
In Reply to: Elizabeth Bott by Buddy Hanna of 458
I am looking for any info on Elizabeth Bott also. Our family has her name as Butt. Then in searching, I have seen it both ways. She and Adam were my GGGGGreat grandparents. The only child I have is my direct line which is a daughter, Mary Agatha (elsewhere recorded as Maria Acuada) May b. 11 Feb. 1792 and d. 8 Sep. 1866. She is my GGGGrandmother. She married David S. Crickenberger b. 18 Nov. 1783in Strasburg, Shenandoah Co., VA and d. 9 May 1855 Mt. Sidney, Augusta Co., VA. That is all I have except I have David and Mary Agatha's children. I need more info on Elizabeth and Adam May if you have any more. Thanks!!
Susan Mullins

There is a Windle Butt on the List of Large Landowners in Rockingham County, 1789 (GenWeb)

Father	Johann Heinrich "Henry" BOTT-2334	
Birth	11 Oct 1731	Sonnenberg, Hessen, Germany
Chr	14 Oct 1731	Sonnenberg, Hessen, Germany
Residence	1748	Philadelphia, Philadelphia, Pennsylvania
Misc	1765	gave 4 pounds to the poor; Lancaster County, Pennsylvania
Misc	1766	gave 3 pounds to the poor; Lancaster County, Pennsylvania
Residence	1770	Maryland
Residence	1774	Rockingham County, Virginia
Misc	1776	gave 2 pounds to the poor; Lancaster County, Pennsylvania
Misc	1777	gave 6 pounds to the poor; Lancaster County, Pennsylvania
Military	1779	paid 2nd Continental tax; Manor, Lancaster, Pennsylvania
Misc	19 Jul 1790	gives consent for Barbara to marry; Augusta County, Virginia
Misc	11 Feb 1791	gave consent for Elizabeth to marry; Augusta County, Virginia
Death	aft 1791	Rockingham County, Virginia
Marriage	29 Jul 1759	First Reformed Church, Lancaster County, Pennsylvania
Father	Johann Emrich BUTT-2337 (-1773)	
Mother	Anna Maria FRESL-2338 (1705-)	

Mother	Margaret CAIN-2335	
Father		
Mother		

Children		
F	Barbara BOTT-2336	
Birth	1770	Taneytown, Carroll, Maryland
Death	1842	Stribling Springs, Augusta, Virginia
Spouse	Christian HUFFMAN-4058 (-)	
Marriage	19 Jul 1790	Augusta County, Virginia
F	ELIZABETH BOTT-2301	
Birth	abt 1774	Maryland
Census	1830	
Census	1840	Rockingham County, Virginia
Death	1851	Rockingham County, Virginia
Spouse	ADAM MAY-2300 (1769-1834)	
Marriage	11 Feb 1791	Augusta County, Virginia

FAMILY NOTES
Marriage (29 July 1759): Per JJ Messersmith notes

FATHER NOTES: Johann Heinrich BOTT-2334
Chr (14 October 1731): per JJ Messersmith notes
Residence (1748): Johan Hendrick Bott arrived on the Ship Hampshire from Rotterdam (qualified 7 Sept 1748) (note in this book says those over age of 16 were marched to the court house immediately to take the oath) per "Names of Foreigners Who Took the Oath of Allegiance to the Province and State of Pennsylvania, 1727-1775, With the Foreign Arrivals, 1786-1808" (available on Google books)
Residence (1770): per daughters' births
Death (after 1791): Per JJ Messersmith notes

MOTHER NOTES: Margaret CAIN-2335
General: Marriage 14 Aug 1759 to Elizabeth Mueller.
Margaret surname may be Cain - Michael Cain took Oath of Allegiance in Pennsylvania

Father	Lawrence "PATRIOT" RAYNES-2312	
Birth	15 Oct 1760	Culpepper County, Virginia
Military	1778	Drafted Rev War ; Orange County, Virginia
Military	1778	DAR PATRIOT-- A104301
Military	1781	Drafted; Rockingham County, Virginia
Military	26 Jun 1781	Battle of Hot Water
Military	Jul 1781	Battle of Jamestown
Military	28 Sep 1781	Battle of Yorktown
Census	1790	Tax List, Orange County, Virginia
Residence	abt 1817	Orange County, Virginia
Census	1820	Rockingham County, Virginia
Military	1832	Pension no. R8623V
Residence	15 Oct 1832	Augusta County, Virginia
Misc	1835	Pensioner ; Rockingham County, Virginia
Death	18 Jul 1837	Rockingham County, Virginia[1]
Marriage	Sep 1782	Virginia
Father	John RAYNES-4093 (1728-)	
Mother	Barbara GOULDEN-4094 (1730-)	

Mother	Mary KNIGHT-4092	
Birth	1766	Rockingham County, Virginia
Residence	1837	Rockingham County, Virginia
Death	1843	Rockingham County, Virginia
Religion		member of Methodist Church; Rockingham County, Virginia[2]
Father		
Mother		

Children		
M	**James RAYNES-4489**	
Birth	abt 1784	Rockingham County, Virginia
Death	abt 1880	Rockingham County, Virginia
Spouse	Zuriah DAVIS-4493 (-)	
Marriage	30 Sep 1802	Rockingham County, Virginia
F	**Ann RAYNES-4492**	
Birth	1790	
F	**Mary Maria RAYNES-4490**	
Birth	1795	Virginia
Death	1860	Rockingham County, Virginia
Spouse	George F. EUTSLER-4491 (-)	
Marriage	15 Sep 1820	Rockingham County, Virginia
F	**Nancy RAYNES-3409**	
Birth	25 Nov 1800	
Death	29 Apr 1845	Virginia
Burial	30 Apr 1845	Central Cemetery, Port Republic, Rockingham County, Virginia
Spouse	Adam MAY Jr.-2305 (1798-1874)	
Marriage	25 Jun 1821	Rockingham County, Virginia
F	**ELIZABETH RAYNES-156**	
Birth	19 Jun 1806	Botetourt County, Virginia
Census	1830	
Census	1840	Rockingham County, Virginia, age 30-40
Census	1850	District 2 and A Half, Augusta County, Virginia
Census	1870	Second Creek, Monroe Co., West Virginia, age 62
Death	28 Aug 1872	Monroe County, West Virginia
Spouse	JACOB MAY-81 (1801-1877)	

1. Rockingham, Virginia, , , , "," ; petition for pension, *Ancestry.com* (: accessed,).
2. Rockingham, Virginia, Virgnia 12,469, Book E, Vol 6, Page 24, , "."

Marriage	3 Jan 1825	Rockingham County, Virginia[3,4]

FAMILY NOTES
Marriage (September 1782): deposition of James Meadows in Rockingham County, Virginia on 4 July 1840
State of Virginia)
Rockingham County) ss
Be it known that on this the 4th day of July, 1840, personally appeared before me a Justice of the Peace in and for the county aforesaid James Meadows aged 78 years and made oath in due form of law that he was well acquainted with Lawrence Raynes and with Mary Raynes (whose maiden name was Mary Knight) and does know that they were married in a very short period after the ending of the Revolutionary Way, deponent cannot now name the day or year when they were married but he is well acquainted with their children and believes their oldest son to be fifty-six or fifty-seven years of age. Deponent has been married himself fully fifty-five years and at the time of his own marriage, the oldest child of Lawrence and Mary Raynes was about one year old. He further states that he was well acquainted with Lawrence Raynes and Mary Raynes his wife from the period of their marriage to the death of Lawrence Raynes, that he lived twenty or thirty years near neighbors to them. He further sayeth not.

James Meadows
(his mark)

Sworn to and subscribed in the day and year last abovementioned before me. I certify that I am well acquainted with James Meadows and he is entitled to full confidence.

Jacob Miller, J.P.

Abraham Roach also swore a statement on 26 Nov 1837 that he believed they were married in late summer of 1782

FATHER NOTES: Lawrence RAYNES-2312
Birth (15 October 1760): Culpepper County created 23 Mar 1748
Military (1778): Under Captain George Waugh and Col. Thomas Barbour
Military (1781): under Captain John Rush of Rockingham

Rockingham County formed in 1778
Military (28 September 1781): The Battle of Yorktown was the battle that ended the Revolutionary War. It took place in 1781 in Yorktown, Virginia, where the British troops were camped out. The Americans and French were fighting against the British Redcoats, who were led by Lord Cornwallis. General Washington and his troops trapped the British with the help of French leaders Count Rochambeau, the Marquis de Lafayette and General Anthony Wayne.
Generals Washington and Rochambeau tricked the British into thinking they would be in New York, but actually they went south to Virginia. They surrounded the British by land and cut off their escape route by the York River. Cornwallis was not able to get reinforcements. General Cornwallis was forced to surrender his troops at Yorktown.
It is said that the British fife and drums played the song *The World Turned Upside Down* when the battle ended because now the colonies belonged to America, not to the British.
Lord North, the British Prime Minister, quit his job after the defeat at Yorktown. The next Prime Minister thought the British should end the war and make peace with America and France.
The British surrendered at Yorktown on October 17, 1781. The agreement to end the Revolutionary War was called the Treaty of Paris which was signed in 1783. That treaty sealed the peace between Great Britain and the new country of the United States.

Yorktown was the largest deep water port between Charleston, SC and Philadelphia, PA and the British established a Customs Collector position to collect the taxes on all goods arriving in the colonies, located in The Custom House, built about 1720. The Custom House was used as barracks for the British troops until the surrender and used by the French troops after the war. Civil War photographer Matthew Brady photographed the ruins of the Custom House in 1865.
Residence (about 1817): Orange County created 20 Sep 1734
Census (1820): Rockingham County created 12 Jan 1778
Residence (15 October 1832): per handwritten letter
Misc (1835): Pensioners on the rolls in 1835 who served as Virginia Militia

"Virginia Militia in the Revolutionary War" by J.T. McAllister, McAllister Publishing Co., Hot Springs, Virginia, c1913.

Death (18 July 1837): per DAR

---

3. Marriage Bond, dated 3 Jan. 1825.
4. John Vogt & T. William Kethley Jr., *Virginia Historic Marriage Register: Rockingham County Marriages, 1778-1850* (Athens, Georgia: n.p., 1984), 151.

MOTHER NOTES: Mary KNIGHT-4092
General: Possible father William (warrant 3606) deceased, John as heir; a Catherine was paid a widow's pension in 1852 (no soldier's name listed)   (Revolutionary War Records, Virginia by Gaius M. Brumbaugh), pg 460

Possible siblings: Mary, Andrew, John, James. (Revolutionary War Records, Virginia by Gaius M. Brumbaugh)

Her last name is listed on the Revolutionary pension application of Lawrence Raynes, her husband

Charles Knight took the Oath in Philadelphia

Raynes, Lawrence – Pension No. R8623. Born Culpepper, about 72 years old in 1832; died July 7, 1837. Drafted from Orange County, Virginia under Captain George Waugh and Colonel Thomas Basborn, not in any engagement. Second tour, three months under Captain John Rush of Rockingham, served near Richard on Bacon Branch, served with Thomas Lewis and John Pence. Third term, three months under Captain George Huston at Williamsburg, fought at Hot Water and Jamestown. Served first under Colonel John Willis and second under Marquis LaFayette, Mr. Thomas Lewis, an officer, and William Davis, siege of York. Served in place of brother Richard Raynes, who was in bad health, served with Chris Ammon, James Meadows, John Taylor, John Pence, Colonel Rush; affidavit by Thomas Lewis, Sr. Declared Minute Book, July 18, 1837 by widow, Mary Knight Raynes, page 32.

--Revolutionary Soldiers, Rockingham County, Virginia; January 1976

Virginia 12,469

Lawrence Raynes

of Rockingham in the State of Virginia
who was a private in the Company commanded
by Captain S. Willis of the Regt. commanded
by Col. Barbour in the Virginia
line for 12 months

Inscribed on the Roll of Virginia
at the rate of 40 Dollars Cents per annum,
to commence on the 4th day of March, 1831.

Certificate of Pension issued the 2d day of May
and sent H. S. Gambill

Arrears to the 4th of March, 1833 — 80
Semiannl. allowance ending 4 Sept. — 20
$100 —

{ Revolutionary Claim, }
{ Act June 7, 1832. }

Recorded by William Miller Clerk.
Book E Vol. 6 Page 24

Letter to A. C. Bryan 31 April 1838
Dead
Paid at the Treasury under
the Act of the 6. April 1838
from 4 March 1837 to the 18
July 1837, the day of his death
Agent notified 21 Aug 1838

State of Virginia and County of Rockingham to wit:

On this 15th day of October, 1822, personally appeared in open court before the Justices of the County Court of Rockingham County now sitting Lawrence Raynes, a resident of the County of Augusta, and State of Virginia, aged about 72 years, who being first duly sworn according to law, doth on his oath make the following declaration in order to obtain the benefit of the Act of Congress dated June 7, 1832.

I, Lawrence Raynes of Augusta County do hereby _____ the following declaration. I was born (I have understood from my parents, for not being able to read or write, they had no written family record) in Culpepper County in Virginia, and am now I suppose about 72 years of age, as nearly as I can judge.

I lived in Orange County when I first entered into the Militia service of the United States. I was drafted in the first call that was made upon Orange County for Militia. I do not remember in what year if was - but I served under Captain George Waugh, and Col. Thomas Basborn (the father of Col. James & Judge Phil Basborn). The service was performed below Richmond, principally in the neighborhood of Williamsburg. This tour was of three months, and I was not in any engagement during it with the enemy. I do not know of any person now living who served in that tour with me and I have not been in Orange for more than 20 years.

My second tour was of three months under Captain John Rush of Rockingham and was principally performed near Richmond, VA. We were encamped on Bacon Branch just above Richmond. This tour I served with ___ Thomas Lewis, (whose deposition is hereto arranged) and John Pence Sr. of Rockingham.

My third tour was also of three months served under Captain George Huston of Rockingham, and was performed principally in that part of the state around Williamsburg. It was a very long service and laborious duty as we were for the most of the time almost constantly marching and generally in the neighborhood of the enemy. In this tour I was in two actions with the British. The first at Hotwater, and the other at Jamestown. In the first action our Brigade was commanded by Col. John Willis and in the second the Marquis La Fayette was our Commander in Chief. In this tour ____Thomas Lewis was one of the officers in our company. I think one William Davis was Lieutenant but Lewis oftener acted as such.

Immediately after I returned home, after the above service, I volunteered again, and went back under Capt. Richard Ragan and served at the Siege of York and was there at the surrender of Lord Cornwallis. I do not remember how long I was in service this tour though I went for three months and stayed until I was discharged and in addition to the four regular tours, I served one under Capt. Baxter of Rockingham, as a member of company to guard a number of Hessian Prisoners from Harrisonburg to Winchester, Virginia. And in the summer after the surrender of Lord Cornwallis, I served another tour of three months under Captain William Smith who commanded the company as far as

Tygart Valley when becoming sick he returned home, and the company was commanded by Neil Cain. This expedition was to the West Fork of the Monongahela against the Indians. I served this tour in the place of my brother, Richard Raynes, who was drafted, but being in bad health, and the Captain refusing to admit that he was unfit for duty, and he being unable to hire a substitute, I voluntarily and without any compensation from him, took his place and served his tour.

This is to the best of my recollection a faithful statement of my services, but being no scholar, not able to write and only able to read a little in print, I cannot remember dates. I was drafted four times, viz the 1st & 2nd & 3rd times, and to guard the Hessian prisoners, volunteered once when Cornwallis was taken, and once took the place of my brother who was drafted. I think I served between 15 and 18 months in all, though I cannot say positively how long it was. I do not remember how long I was under Baxter and perhaps I may have been discharged before my three months expired after Cornwallis was taken, but I am certain that I entered in service five times for three months each and that I served every time until the company I belonged to was regularly discharged.

Of the Continental Officers who acted with the troops I served with, I remember Col. Denk, Col. Willis, Gen Muchlenberg, Marquis La Fayette and Gen Washington. I do not remember that I was given any written discharge. I remember several persons now living that I served with, as Christopher Ammon, James Meadows, John Taylor, John Pence, Col. Rush and others who are now living, but I have not been able to see any of them except Thomas Lewis (whose testimony is hereto arranged) as I am too old and inform (being scarcely able to walk from a very bad rupture) to walk in order to get their testimony and too poor to procure any mode of conveyance.

I do hereby relinquish every claim whatever to a pension or annuity except the present, and declare that my name is not on the pension roll of the agency of any state.

Signed,

Lawrence (X his mark) Raynes

State of Virginia and County of Rockingham to wit:

On this 15th day of October 1832 personally appeared in open Court, before the Justices of the County Court of Rockingham County, now sitting, Lawrence Raynes, a resident of the County of Augusta, and State of Virginia aged about 72 years, who being first duly sworn according to law, doth on his oath make the following declaration, in order to obtain the benefit of the act of Congress passed June 7th 1832.

I Lawrence Raynes of Augusta County do hereby certify the following declaration. I was born (I have understood from my parents, for not being able to read or write they had no written family record) in Culpepper county, in Virginia, and am now I suppose about 72 years of age, as nearly as I can judge. I lived in Orange County when I first entered into the militia service of the United States. I was drafted in the first call that was made from Orange County for militia. I do not remember in what year it was — but I served under captain George Waugh, and Col. Thomas Barbour (the father Col. James & Judge Phil Barbour). The service was performed below Richmond principally in the neighborhood of Williamsburg. This tour was of three months, and I was not in any engagement during it with the enemy. I do not know of any person now living who served in that tour with me, and I have not been in Orange for more than 20 years. My second tour was of three months under Captain John Reid of Rockingham, & was principally performed near Richmond &c. we were encamped on Bacon branch just above Richmond. In this tour I served with Mr. Thomas Lewis, (whose deposition is hereto annexed) and John Pence Senr. of Rockingham. My third tour was also of three months served under captain George Dexton of Rockingham, & was performed principally in that part of the state round about Williamsburg

It was a very severe and laborious duty, as we were for most of the time, almost constantly marching & generally in the neighborhood of the enemy.— In this tour I was in two actions with the British. The first at Botwater, and the other at James Town— In the first action our Brigade was commanded Colo. John Willis,— and in the Second the Marquis La Fayette was our Commander in Chief.— In this tour Mr. Thomas Lewis was one of the Officers in our Company— I think one William Lewis was Lieutenant, but W. Lewis often acted as such.— Immediately after I returned home, after the above services I volunteered again, and went back under Capt. Richard Ragan & served at the Siege of York, and was there at the Surrender of Lord Cornwallis.— I do not remember how long I was in service this tour. Though I went for three months and staid until I was discharged— and in addition to the four regular tours, I served one under Capt. Bogles of Rockingham, as a member of company to guard a number of Hessian Prisoners from Harrisonburg to Winchester Va.— And in the Summer after the Surrender of Lord Cornwallis I served another tour of three months under Captain William Smith (who commanded the company as far as Tygart's Valley when becoming sick he returned home, & the company was commanded by Neil Cain) This expedition was to the West Fork of the Monongalela against the Indians.— I served this tour in the place of my brother Richard Ragan, who was drafted, but being in bad health, & the Captain refusing to admit that he was unfit for duty, & he being unable to hire a substitute I voluntarily & without any compensation from him, took his place & served his tour.— This is to the best of my recollection a faithful statement of my services,— but being no scholar, not able to write and only able to read a little in print, I cannot remember dates.— I was drafted four times, viz. the 1st & 2nd tours, & to guard the Hessian Prisoners.— Volunteer ed once when Cornwallis was taken, and once took the place of my brother who was drafted. — I think I served between 15 & 18 months in all, — though I cannot say positively how long it was — I do not remember how long I was under Baptist, — and perhaps I may have been discharged before my three months service after Cornwallis was taken, but I am certain that I entered in service five times for three months each, and that I served every time untill the company I belonged to was regularly discharged. — Of the Continental Officers who acted with the troops I served with, I remember Col Lewis — Col Willis — Genl Muhlenberg — Marquis La Fayette, & Genl Washington, — I do not remember that I ever had any written discharge — I remember several persons now living that I served with, as Christopher Simmon — James Meadows — John Taylor — John Pence — Col Rush, & others who are now living, but I have not been able to see any of them except Mr Thos Lewis (whose testimony is hereto annexed) as I am too old & infirm (being scarcely able to walk from a very bad rupture) to walk in order to get their testimony, and too poor to procure any mode of conveyance.

I do hereby relinquish every claim whatever to a pension or annuity except the present, and declare that my name is not on the pension roll of the agency of any state —

     Signed
      Lawrence Raynes
       his mark

I Thomas Lewis Senr of Rockingham County in Virginia do hereby certify that I distinctly remember that Lawrence Raynes did serve a tour of militia duty as he states, under Captain John Rush — the service was performed in the year 1778 I think — and also, a tour as he states under Captain George

Bibliography

(2006, April). Retrieved Aug 2011, from Rockingham County, Virginia VAGenWeb Project: http://www.rootsweb.ancestry.com/~varockin/history2.htm

Affairs, D. o. (n.d.). *VA History in Brief, Dept of Veterans Affairs*. Retrieved August 2011, from http://www.va.gov/opa/publications/archives/docs/history_in_brief.pdf

Census, U. F. (1860). Retrieved September 2011, from Ancestry.com: http://search.ancestry.com/search/category.aspx?cat=35

Crumpacker, G. W. (1977). *The Complete History of Sullivan County, Missouri 1836-1900*. History Publications, Inc.

Dunker, C. (2011, April 16). *The Beatrice Daily Sun*. Retrieved August 2011, from http://beatricedailysun.com/news/article_f382f592-67cb-11e0-a3f8-001cc4c03286.html

Foote, S. (1998). *The Civil War: A Narrative*. New York: Time Life Inc.

Kiner, F. F. (1863). *One Year's Soldiering*. E. H. Thomas, Printer.

Reed, D. W. (1903). *The Battle of Shiloh and the Organizations Engaged*. Washington, D.C.: Government Printing Office.

Stewart, P. (2004). *History of the 23rd Missouri Volunteer Infantry and the Battle of Shiloh, April 6-7, 1862*. Retrieved August 2011, from USGenWeb Project: http://www.rootsweb.ancestry.com/~moharris/shilohnarrative.html

The Valley of the Shadow. (n.d.). Retrieved August 2011, from Franklin County: General Information for Soldiers and their Heirs, Entitled to Old Bounty: http://valley.lib.virginia.edu/mem/FM0064

Illustration References

Cover and interior photo of Fountain May – original owned by author

Interior graphic – Union Flag in form of a shield – https://www.loc.gov/item/2011648675

p. 1 – Example of a grist mill – https://en.wikipedia.org/wiki/Hope_Park

p. 2 – The Great Valley Road – drawn by author

p. 6 – Tent Camp – https://www.pinterest.com/pin/329466528965247312/

p. 8 – Shiloh Meeting House – http://shilohdiscussiongroup.com/index.php?/gallery/album/29-roger39s-album/

p. 9 – Pittsburg Landing – from "The Soldier in Our Civil War", Mottelay & Campbell-Copeland, 1890; Vol 1, p 266-7

p. 11 – Battle Map – from "The Soldier in Our Civil War", Mottelay & Campbell-Copeland, 1890; Vol 1, p 263

p. 12 – Troops Fleeing – http://cdn.loc.gov/service/pnp/cph/3b00000/3b07000/3b07100/3b07178r.jpg

p. 13 – The Hornet's Nest – (Battle of Shiloh, by Thure de Thulstrup); https://en.wikipedia.org/wiki/Battle_of_Shiloh

p. 17 – Union Prison at Cahawba – Hawes, Jesse. Cahaba, A Story of Captive Boys in Blue. New York: Burr Printing House, 1888. Public Domain, https://commons.wikimedia.org/w/index.php?curid=5465924

p. 18 – Fountain May's route – drawn by author

p. 19 – Camp Oglethorpe Prisoners – From Life and Death in Rebel Prisons by Robert H. Kellogg, 1866

p. 21 – Bone Ring – https://www.pinterest.com

p. 23 – Emaciated Union Soldier who survived – https://en.wikipedia.org/wiki/Andersonville_National_Historic_Site

p. 24 – Andersonville Cemetery – Emaze.com

p. 38 – Virginia May's gravesite – photographed by author

p. 39 – Memorial stone – photographed by author

p. 59 – Shiloh Battlefield markers – (National Park Service) http://www.shilohbattlefield.org/results.asp?varCWUNIT=UMO0023RI&Submit=Submit

p. 62 – Major John McCullough – https://sites.google.com/site/23rdmov/

p. 63 – Col. Jacob Tindall – https://sites.google.com/site/23rdmov/

p. 64 – Brig Gen Benjamin Prentiss – https://en.wikipedia.org/wiki/Battle_of_Shiloh

p. 65 – Prentiss Headquarters Marker – (National Park Service) http://www.shilohbattlefield.org/officerresults.asp?varOFFICERNAME=PRENBM&Submit=Submit

p. 67 – Major Gen Ulysses S Grant – Engraved, full-page portrait of General Grant from Harper's Weekly, Dec. 9, 1865

Contact the Author

Often readers like to contact the author to inquire about additional research either on the May Family or other family members. The author, Flora McCarty, welcomes readers to contact her. Please email Flora at: florabegora@comcast.net. Her extensive genealogy research may help you uncover family history not previously found.